The E Myth Attorney

The **E** Myth
Attorney

*Why Most Legal
Practices Don't Work
and What to Do About It*

MICHAEL E. GERBER
ROBERT ARMSTRONG
SANFORD M. FISCH

WILEY

John Wiley & Sons, Inc.

Published by John Wiley & Sons, Inc., Hoboken, New Jersey.
Published simultaneously in Canada.

For general information on our other products and services or for technical support, please contact our Customer Care Department within the United States at (800) 762-2974, outside the United States at (317) 572-3993 or fax (317) 572-4002.

Wiley also publishes its books in a variety of electronic formats. Some content that appears in print may not be available in electronic books. For more information about Wiley products, visit our web site at www.wiley.com.

Library of Congress Cataloging-in-Publication Data:

Gerber, Michael E.
  The e-myth attorney: why most legal practices don't work and what to do about it / Michael E. Gerber, Robert Armstrong, Sandford Fisch.
    p. cm.
  Includes bibliographical references and index.
  ISBN 978-0-470-50365-2 (cloth)
  1. Practice of law—United States. 2. Law offices—United States—Management.
I. Armstrong, Robert. II. Fisch, Sanford. III. Title.
  KF300.G47 2010
  340.023'73—dc22

                                                              2009052162

Printed in the United States of America.

10 9 8 7 6 5 4 3 2 1

To Luz Delia, whose heart expands mine,
whose soul inspires mine,
whose boldness reaches for the stars, thank you,
forever, for being, truly mine . . .

—Michael E. Gerber

CONTENTS

A WORD ABOUT THIS BOOK

Michael E. Gerber

My first E-Myth book was published in 1985. It was called *The E-Myth: Why Most Small Businesses Don't Work and What to Do About It.* Since that book, and the company I created to provide business development services to its many readers, millions have read *The E-Myth,* and the book that followed it called *The E-Myth Revisited,* and tens of thousands have participated in our E-Myth Mastery programs.

The co-authors of this book, *The E-Myth Attorney,* Robert Armstrong and Sanford (Sandy) Fisch, were two of those more than enthusiastic readers, and, as a direct result of their enthusiasm, their estate planning legal practice became one of those clients. Both gentlemen became, over the years, very close friends of mine.

This book is two things: the product of my lifelong work conceiving, developing, and growing the E-Myth way into a business model that has been applied to every imaginable kind of company in the world, as well as a product of Robert and Sandy's extraordinary experience and success applying the E-Myth to the development of their equally extraordinary legal enterprise, the American Academy of Estate Planning Attorneys.

So it was that one day, while sitting with my muse, which I think of as my inner voice, and which many who know me think of as "here he goes again!" that I thought about the creation of an entire series of E-Myth vertical books. That series, of which this is the first, would be co-authored by experts in every industry who had

ix

successfully applied my E-Myth principles to the extreme development of a practice—a very small company—with the intent of growing it nationwide, and even worldwide, which is what Robert and Sandy had in mind as they began to discover the almost infinite range of opportunities provided by thinking the E-Myth way.

Upon seeing the possibilities of this new idea, I immediately went to Robert and Sandy and shared my excitement with them. Not surprisingly, they said, "Let's do it!" And so we did.

Welcome to the first of those many vertical market E-Myth expert books, *The E-Myth Attorney: Why Most Legal Practices Don't Work and What to Do About It.*

Read it, enjoy it, and let us—Robert, Sandy, and I—help you apply the E-Myth to the re-creation, development, and extreme growth of your legal practice into an enterprise that you can be justifiably proud of.

To your life, your wisdom, and the life and success of your clients, I wish you good reading.

—Michael E. Gerber
Founder–Chairman
Michael E. Gerber Companies, Inc.
Carlsbad, California
www.michaelegerber.com/attorney

A NOTE FROM ROBERT AND SANDY

Aword of warning before we get started: Reading this book
and implementing its message will transform the way you
practice law and, in the process, may even change your life.
We are lawyers and over 20 years ago a close friend and successful
financial advisor gave each of us a book by Michael E. Gerber, *The
E-Myth: Why Most Small Businesses Don't Work and What to Do
About It*. No one, except maybe Michael E. Gerber, could have
imagined what followed.

The "we" refers to us, Robert Armstrong and Sanford M. Fisch,
law and business partners for more than twenty years. Sandy vividly
remembers placing his copy of the book in his briefcase as he was
leaving our San Diego office for the airport for one of his regular trips
to one of our northern California law offices. He spent three busy
days in those offices and never had a minute to even open the book.

Finally, as he settled into his seat on the return flight home to
San Diego, he opened the book and read the inscription our friend
had scribbled on the inside cover, "Read, Re-read, Enjoy!" Sandy
still has that book and sometimes opens it to look at the notes he
made that fateful evening. Once he started to read, he never
stopped. The flight was only an hour and half but he made a real
dent in the book. Once home, he just continued the journey. This
book's message spoke to him directly, and he was compelled to finish
it, make his notes, plot his course of action, and anxiously look

forward to a discussion with Robert because he knew we were on the same journey.

The next morning was monumental because when we got to the office, each of us had finished the book. We compared notes, had animated discussions and knew exactly what we needed to do. Our first priority was to begin "working on the business" not just "work in business." You see, that's one of the many extraordinary principles that jumped out for both of us. We came to understand that this idea of a legal practice as a business was something bigger and more importantly, separate from ourselves, a living entity that we could intentionally design, mold, and create.

Over the years since our first introduction to Michael's book we have moved beyond merely understanding his message to living it day by day. The E-Myth point of view was the beginning of the framework for retooling our successful law practice and ultimately building a national organization to teach attorneys how to become not only consummate legal technicians but also savvy business leaders. The extraordinary thing about the E-Myth point of view is that it applies universally to all businesses—yes, even the business of practicing law! We know this firsthand and have coached hundreds of lawyers all over the country for the past 17 years.

As experienced lawyers ourselves, and being intimately familiar with how lawyers think, we know some of you are already muttering that it is different for you and your law practice because. . . . You fill in the blank. Believe us, we've heard every reason why these principles won't work in Utah, Vermont, Tennessee, Montana, Illinois, and, of course, New York City! We've heard how it can't apply to a litigation practice, bankruptcy law, or even tax and estate planning. However, we've seen these timeless principles work wonders in any locale or any kind of practice area.

To benefit from this book, you've got to clear away all those old ideas that your practice is somehow different, because this type of thinking keeps most attorneys stuck in the daily grind of, as Michael E. Gerber says, "doing it, doing it, and doing it." The real key is to start thinking of your practice as a business that provides legal services. If you don't want a "business," then give this book to someone else. Make no mistake about it, this book is about business and, more specifically, how you can turn your law practice into a business that ultimately has a life apart from you.

As lawyers ourselves, we understand the evolution of the dream from your first day of law school. We understand how the dream peaked as you passed the bar and were sworn in. We remember the heady days of living the dream in your early days of practice. And we understand the moment when your dream comes face to face with the harsh reality of the long hours, tedious paperwork, and the nonstop conflict required by both the beginning attorney and the journeyman practitioner.

Unfortunately, after many years grinding it out, we also understand the all-too-common cynicism that replaces that dream. In fact, for most, the dream that once was a guiding star is now just a distant and foolish memory.

The unique aspect of law is that it is an honorable professional practice, the combination of knowledge and experience—the intellectual in the marketplace. One is always gaining more experience and adding it to the unlimited knowledge about a particular topic. That alone is a full-time job. However, add to that the skills required to run a profitable law firm and it morphs into something more complex, exponentially more time consuming, and more importantly, something no one ever taught us in law school.

So here we are down the road as lawyers. In our cases, Robert has over thirty-four years and Sandy more than thirty as lawyers. We've seen it all and know exactly what's needed to get you out of the unfulfilled practice trap. Our initial guiding light was the book we received years ago. Now we join with Michael, as E-Myth attorneys, to help you see the practice of law in a whole new light with a revolutionary point of view.

If you are ready to be a serious student and fully commit to changing how you think about your practice, turn the pages and get ready for the ride of your lives. Granted, this is by no means the final word on each of these topics, but it is a grand introduction to a new way of thinking. For us, the reading of the original E-Myth book was a defining moment in our lives. We hope that our book will be as significant for you.

And as someone once said to us, "Read, Re-read, Enjoy!"

—Robert Armstrong and Sanford M. Fisch
The American Academy of Estate Planning Attorneys
San Diego, CA
www.michaelegerber.com/attorney

PREFACE

Michael E. Gerber

I am not an attorney, although I have helped thousands of attorneys reinvent their legal practices over the past 35 years. I like to think of myself as a thinker, maybe even a dreamer. Yes, I like to *do* things. But before I jump in and get my hands dirty, I prefer to think through what I'm going to do and figure out the best way to do it. I imagine the impossible, dream big, and then try to figure out how the impossible can become the possible. After that, it's about how to turn the possible into reality.

Over the years, I've made it my business to study how things work and how people work—specifically, how things and people work best together to produce optimum results. That means creating an organization that can do great things and achieve more than any other organization can. Or, in the case of attorneys, a legal practice that surpasses the competition and provides high standards of service, high income, and equally high job satisfaction to all who work at the firm.

The end product has been a series of books that I've authored— *The E-Myth* books—as well as a company, E-Myth Worldwide, which I founded in 1977, Chief Dreamer Enterprises, in 2005, and Michael E. Gerber Companies in 2009. For over 30 years, my first company, E-Myth Worldwide, has helped tens of thousands of small business owners, including many attorneys, reinvent the way that they do business by (1) rethinking the purpose of their legal practices, and (2) imagining how they could fulfill their purpose in innovative ways.

Many attorneys view practice management as an unwelcome burden that distracts them from their main responsibility of representing the interests of their clients, creating and closing transactions, winning cases, and not least, getting paid. Yet practice management—what I like to call *practice liberation*—can be just as exciting (and lucrative) as a jury returning a record verdict in your client's favor.

This book is about how to produce the best results as a real-world attorney in the development, expansion, and, yes, *liberation* of your practice. In the process, you will come to understand what the practice of law—as a *business*—is, and what it isn't.

This book, intentionally small, is about big ideas. The topics we'll be discussing in this book are the very issues that attorneys face daily in their practice. You know what they are: people, money, management, and many more. My aim is to help you begin the exciting process of totally transforming the way you do business. (And whether attorneys want to admit it or not, they are indeed doing business. Some not as well as others, despite the long hours they log.) As such, I'm confident that *The E-Myth Attorney* could well be the most important book on the practice of law as a business you'll ever read.

Unlike other books on the market, my goal is not to tell you how to do the work you do. Instead, I want to share with you the E-Myth philosophy as a way to revolutionize the way you *think* about the work you do. I'm convinced that this new way of thinking is something attorneys everywhere must adopt in order for their legal practice to flourish during these trying times. I call it strategic thinking, as opposed to tactical thinking.

In strategic thinking, also called systems thinking, you, the attorney, will begin to think about your entire practice—the broad scope of it—instead of focusing on its individual parts. You will begin to see the end game (perhaps for the first time) rather than just the day-to-day routine that's consuming you—the endless, draining work I call "doing it, doing it, doing it" (followed by "billing it, billing it, billing it, and hoping you actually get paid).

Understanding strategic thinking will enable you to create a practice that becomes a successful business, with the potential to flourish as an even more successful enterprise. But in order for you to accomplish this, your practice, your business, and certainly your enterprise must work *apart* from you instead of *because* of you.

The E-Myth philosophy says that a highly successful legal practice can grow into a highly successful legal business, which in turn can become the foundation for an inordinately successful legal enterprise that runs smoothly and efficiently *without* the attorney having to be in the office for 16 billable hours a day, six days a week.

So what is the "E-Myth," exactly? The E-Myth is short for the Entrepreneurial Myth, which says that most businesses fail to fulfill their potential because most people starting their own business are not entrepreneurs at all. They're actually what I call *technicians suffering from an entrepreneurial seizure.* When technicians suffering from an entrepreneurial seizure—in this case, attorneys—start a legal practice of their own, they almost always end up working themselves into a frenzy, going straight from one case to the next, and hardly ever taking a break. They're burning the candle at both ends, fueled by too much coffee and too little sleep, and most of the time, they can't even stop to think. If this sounds familiar, keep reading.

In short, the E-Myth says that most attorneys don't own a true business—most own a job disguised as a legal practice. They're doing it, doing it, doing it, hoping like hell to get some time off, but never figuring out how to get their business to run without them. And if your business doesn't run well without you, what happens when you can't be in two places at once? Ultimately, your practice will fail.

It's happening throughout the world even as you're reading these words. In today's economy, fewer and fewer attorneys are being hired by big law firms, which means that around 85% end up hanging out their own shingle or toiling in a small law firm at some point in their career. But as long as law schools neglect to teach courses on the *business* of law, a large percentage of these small firms and solo practitioners are going to fail. No matter how much an attorney may know about tort, intellectual property (IP), domestic relations, tax, estate planning, criminal law, contract law, or any of the other subspecialities—and you could very well be an expert in any or all of these fields—none of that expertise is in itself sufficient to build a successful business.

The good news is that you don't have to be among the statistics of failure in the legal profession. The E-Myth philosophy I am about to share with you in this book has been successfully applied to thousands of legal practices just like yours with extraordinary results. In fact my co-authors Robert and Sandy, through the American Academy of Estate Planning Attorneys, have for 17 years regularly implemented this philosophy in law firms across the country.

The key to transforming your practice—and your life—is to grasp the profound difference between going to work *on* your practice (systems thinker) and going to work *in* your practice (tactical thinker). In other words, it's the difference between going to work *on* your practice as an entrepreneur and going to work in your practice as an attorney.

The two are not mutually exclusive. In fact, they are essential to each other. The problem with most legal practices is that the systems thinker—the entrepreneur—is completely absent. And so is the vision.

The E-Myth philosophy says that the key to transforming your practice into a successful enterprise is knowing how to transform yourself from a successful legal technician (attorney) into a successful legal technician-manager-entrepreneur. In the process, everything you do in your legal practice will be transformed. The door is then open to turning it into the kind of practice it should be—a practice, a business, an enterprise of pure joy!

It's my thesis that the E-Myth not only *can* work for you, but that it *will* work for you. And in the process it will give you an entirely new experience of your business and beyond.

To your future and your life. Good reading.

ACKNOWLEDGMENTS

Our deep gratitude to the financial advisor, friend and visionary, himself—Aubrey Morrow, CFP. Thanks again for insisting that we read the E-Myth book.

Also, thanks to all the attorneys we've had the privilege to work with, including the extraordinary Members of the American Academy of Estate Planning Attorneys.

And finally, our heartfelt thanks to the amazing staff at the Academy who have brought our vision to life.

—Robert Armstrong
—Sanford M. Fisch

INTRODUCTION

Michael E. Gerber

In August 2009, *The American Lawyer* published the results of an extensive survey in which 83% of law firm associates expressed significant anxiety about losing their jobs. Another 46% said they had seen a drop-off in their workload since the recession. And an additional 56% of respondents admitted to being troubled by a lack of financial transparency and mishandling of communications in their firm, which more often than not led to layoffs, pay cuts, and furloughs, and even the collapse of some firms.

Unfortunately, I can't say I'm surprised. Most attorneys I've met are beleaguered, frustrated, and worried. In the midst of such trying economic times, many are currently asking themselves, "Why in the world did I become a lawyer?"

And it isn't just a money problem. After thirty-five years of working with small businesses, a good many of them legal practices, I'm convinced that the malaise and dissatisfaction experienced by countless attorneys is not just about money. Money may be a part of the equation, but it's much more than that.

It's no secret that the life of a legal professional today is one of continuous and often soul-crushing frustration. Despite their extensive knowledge and expertise, many attorneys find themselves buried under a mountain of paperwork and a battery of briefs. Any joy or sense of justice they once derived from their chosen profession disappeared long ago—if it ever existed at all.

What's the real reason for this anxiety? Unlike what others may tell you, it's not the recession. The financial crisis that our country is facing certainly hasn't made things any better, but the problem started long before the economy tanked. Let's dig a little deeper. Let's go back to law school.

Can you remember that far back? You might not want to revisit those three years of terror mixed with boredom, but let's go back there for a moment. You probably had some great professors who helped you become the fine attorney you are. It's universally accepted that law schools are great at teaching students how to understand the law and think like a lawyer. But they don't teach many of the skills needed to be a successful lawyer, and they certainly don't teach what it takes to build a successful legal enterprise.

Obviously, something is seriously wrong. The education that legal professionals receive in school doesn't go far enough, deep enough, or broad enough. Law schools don't teach you how to relate to the *enterprise* of law or to the *business* of law; they only teach you how to relate to the *practice* of law. In other words, they merely teach you how to be an *effective* rather than a *successful* attorney.

That's why there are myriad attorneys today who are effective, but very few successful ones. Although a successful attorney must be effective, an effective attorney does not have to be—and in most cases isn't—successful.

An effective attorney is capable of executing his or her legal duties with as much certainty and professionalism as possible.

A successful attorney, on the other hand, works balanced hours, has little stress, enjoys rich and rewarding relationships with friends and family, and has an economic life that is diverse, fulfilling, and shows a continuous return on investment.

A successful attorney finds time and ways to give back to the community but at little cost to his or her sense of ease.

A successful attorney is a leader who has more to teach clients than just legal wisdom; a sage; a rich person (in the broadest sense of the word); a strong father, mother, wife, or husband; a friend, teacher, mentor, and spiritually grounded human being; and a person who lives beyond the *letter* of the law to fully exemplify the *spirit* of the law.

I know what you're thinking. Sightings of successful attorneys, thus defined, are approximately as rare as sightings of the Loch Ness monster.

So let's go back to the original question: Why did you become an attorney? Were you striving to just be an effective one, or did you dream about real and resounding success? Was it about bringing justice to those who place their trust in you, or was it about struggling twice a month to have enough cash flow to meet the firm's payroll demands?

I don't know how you've answered that question in the past, but I am confident that once you understand the strategic thinking laid out in this book, you will answer it differently in the future.

If the ideas here are going to be of value to you, it's critical that you begin to look at yourself in a different, more productive way. I am suggesting that you go beyond the mere technical aspects of your daily job as an attorney, and begin instead to think strategically about your legal practice as both a business and an enterprise.

I often say that most *practices* don't work—the people who own them do. In other words, most legal practices are jobs for the attorneys who own them. Does this sound familiar? The attorney, overcome by an entrepreneurial seizure, has started his or her own practice, become his or her own boss, and now works for a lunatic!

The result: The attorney is running out of time, patience, and ultimately money. Not to mention paying the worst price anyone can pay for the inability to understand what a true practice is, what a true business is, and what a true enterprise is—the price of his or her life.

In this book I'm going to make the case for why you should think differently about what you do and why you do it. It isn't just the future of your legal practice that hangs in the balance. It's the future of your life.

The *E-Myth Attorney* is an exciting departure from my other sole-authored books. In this book, E-Myth experts—professionals who have successfully applied the E-Myth to the development of their legal practice—are sharing their secrets about how they achieved extraordinary results using the E-Myth paradigm. In addition to the time-tested E-Myth strategies and systems I'll be sharing with you, you'll benefit from the wisdom, guidance, and practical tips provided by experienced attorneys who've been in your shoes.

The problems that afflict legal practices today don't only exist in law; the same problems are confronting every organization of every size, in every industry in every country in the world. *The E-Myth Attorney* is the first in a new series of E-Myth expert books in all industries that will serve as a launching pad for Michael E. Gerber Partners™ to bring a legacy of expertise to the world of small, struggling businesses. This series will offer an exciting opportunity to understand and apply the significance of E-Myth methodology in both theory and practice to businesses in need of development and growth.

The E-Myth says that only by conducting your business in a truly innovative and independent way will you ever realize the unmatched joy that comes from creating a truly independent business, a business that works *without* you rather than *because* of you.

The E-Myth says that it is only by learning the difference between the work of a *business* and the business of *work* that attorneys will be freed from the predictable and often overwhelming tyranny of the unprofitable, unproductive routine that consumes them on a daily basis.

The E-Myth says that what will make the ultimate difference between the success or failure of your legal practice is first and foremost how you *think* about your business, as opposed to how hard you work in it.

So, let's think it through together. Let's think about those things—work, people, money, and time—that dominate the world of attorneys everywhere.

Let's talk about planning. About growth. About management. About getting a life!

Let's think about improving you and your family's life through the development of an extraordinary practice. About getting a life that's *yours*.

CHAPTER

1

The Story of Edward and Abigail

Michael E. Gerber

*To understand the heart and mind of a person, look not at what he has
already achieved, but at what he aspires to.*
—Kahlil Gibran, *Sand and Foam*

E very business is a family business. To ignore this truth is to
court disaster.

This is true whether or not family members actually
work in the business. Whatever their relationship with the business,
every member of an attorney's family will be greatly affected by the
decisions the attorney makes about the business.

Unfortunately, attorneys tend to compartmentalize their lives
unless family members are actively involved in their legal practice.
Attorneys see their practice as separate from their family, and
concepts like attorney–client privilege only reinforce that belief.
They view their practice as a profession—what they do—and
therefore none of their family's business.

1

"This doesn't concern you," says the attorney to her husband.

"I leave business at the office and my family at home," says the attorney, with blind conviction.

And with equal conviction, I say, "Not true!"

In actuality, your family and legal practice are inextricably linked to one another. What's happening in your practice is also happening at home. Consider the following and ask yourself whether each one is true:

- If you're angry at work, you're also angry at home.
- If you're out of control in your legal practice, you're equally out of control at home.
- If you're having trouble with money in your practice, you're also having trouble with money at home.
- If you have communication problems in your practice, you're also having communication problems at home.
- If you don't trust in your practice, you don't trust at home.
- If you're secretive in your practice, you're equally secretive at home.

And you're paying a huge price for each of these! The truth is that your practice and your family are one—and you're the link. Or you should be. Because if you try to keep your practice and your family apart, if your practice and your family are strangers, you will effectively create two separate worlds that can never wholeheartedly serve each other. Two worlds that split each other apart.

Let me tell you the story of Edward and Abigail.

Edward and Abigail met their senior year in college. While participating in a campus party celebrating the 200-year birthday of the U.S. Constitution, they sat next to each other and talked for hours. They were both pre-law and passionately committed to improving the nation's justice system. They'd watched as America's trust in its politicians was slowly eroded by a series of political scandals, beginning with Watergate in the 1970s and continuing into the 1980s with the FBI Abscam sting in which one senator, five members of the House of Representatives, and several other high-ranking government officials were convicted of accepting bribes.

Edward was impressed by Abigail's extensive social work in the community, and Abigail thought Edward was the most dynamic man she had ever met. It wasn't long before they were engaged and planning their future together.

While Edward attended law school, Abigail pursued a master's degree in social work. Over the next few years, the couple worked various jobs to keep their finances afloat. They were often exhausted and struggled to make ends meet, but they were committed to what they were doing and to each other.

After receiving his J.D. degree and passing the state bar, Edward went to work for a medium-sized law firm. Soon afterward, the couple had their first daughter, and Abigail decided to take some time off from her job as a social worker to be a stay-at-home mom. Those were good years. They dearly loved each other, were active members of their church, participated in community organizations, and spent quality time together. All in all, they considered themselves one of the most fortunate families they knew.

But work became troublesome. Edward grew increasingly frustrated with the way the firm was run. "I want to go into business for myself," he announced one night at the dinner table. "I want to start my own practice."

Edward and Abigail spent many nights talking about the move. Was it something they could afford? Did Edward really have the skills necessary to make a legal practice a success? Were there enough clients to go around? What impact would such a move have on their lifestyle, on their daughter, on their relationship? They asked all the questions they thought they needed to answer before going into business for themselves . . . but they never really drew up a concrete plan.

Finally, tired of talking and confident that he could handle whatever he might face, Edward committed to starting his own legal practice. Because she loved and supported him, Abigail agreed, offering her own commitment to help in any way she could. So Edward quit his job at the firm, took out a second mortgage on their home, and leased a small office.

In the beginning, things went well. A building boom had hit the town, and new families were pouring into the area. Edward had no trouble getting new clients. His practice expanded, quickly outgrowing his office.

Within a year, Edward had employed two full-time paralegals. He also hired a bookkeeper named Rebecca to take care of the money and a receptionist named Emily to handle the telephone and administrative responsibilities. Edward was ecstatic with the progress his young practice had made. He celebrated by taking his wife and daughter on vacation to Maui.

Of course, managing a business was more complicated and time consuming than working for someone else. Edward not only supervised all the jobs his people did, but he was continually looking for work to keep everyone busy. When he wasn't scanning legal journals to stay abreast of what was going on in his field, he was editing briefs, revising client contracts, and wading through endless piles of paperwork. He also found himself spending more and more time on the telephone, mostly dealing with client complaints and nurturing relationships.

As the months went by and more and more clients came through the door, Edward had to spend even more time just trying to keep his head above water.

By the end of its second year, the practice, now employing four full-time and two part-time people, had moved to a larger office downtown. The demands on Edward's time had grown with the practice.

He began leaving home earlier in the morning and returning home later at night. He rarely saw his daughter anymore. For the most part, Edward was resigned to the problem. He saw the hard work as essential to building the "sweat equity" he had long heard about.

Money was also becoming a problem for Edward. Although the practice was growing like crazy, money always seemed scarce when it was really needed. He had discovered that clients were often slow to pay.

When Edward had worked at someone else's law firm, he had been paid twice a month; in his own practice, he often had to wait—sometimes for months. He was still owed money on cases he had completed more than 90 days before.

Of course, no matter how slowly Edward got paid, he still had to pay *his* people. This became a relentless problem. Edward often felt like a juggler dancing on a tightrope. A fire burned in his stomach day and night.

To make matters worse, Edward began to feel that Abigail was insensitive to his troubles. Not that he often talked to his wife about the practice. "Business is business" was Edward's mantra. "It's my responsibility to handle things at the office and Abigail's responsibility to take care of our daughter, the house, and me."

Abigail's seeming lack of understanding rankled Edward. Didn't she see that he had a practice to take care of? That he was doing it all for his family? Apparently not.

As time went on, Edward became even more consumed by his practice. Not surprisingly, Abigail grew more frustrated by her husband's lack of communication and increasingly long hours. She'd put her own social work on hold to focus on their family, and now her husband was hardly ever at home. Their relationship grew tense and strained. The rare moments they *were* together were more often than not peppered by long silences—a far cry from the fiery discussions and impassioned dreaming that had characterized their relationship's early days.

Meanwhile, Rebecca, the bookkeeper, was becoming a problem for Edward. Rebecca never seemed to have the financial information Edward needed to make decisions about payroll, client billing, and general operating expenses, let alone how much money was available for Edward and Abigail's living expenses.

When questioned, Rebecca would shift her gaze to her feet and say, "Listen, Edward, I've got a lot more to do around here than you can imagine. It'll take a little more time. Just don't press me, okay?"

Overwhelmed by his own work, Edward usually backed off. The last thing Edward wanted was to upset Rebecca and have to do the books himself. He could also empathize with what Rebecca was going through, given the practice's growth over the past year.

Late at night in his office, Edward would sometimes recall his first years out of law school. He missed the simple life he and his family had shared. Then, as quickly as the thoughts came, they would vanish. He had work to do and no time for daydreaming. "Having my own law practice is a great thing," he would remind himself. "I simply have to apply myself, as I did in school, and get on with the job. I have to work as hard as I always have when something needed to get done."

Edward began to live most of his life inside his head. He began to distrust his people. They never seemed to work hard enough or to care about his practice as much as he did. If he wanted to get something done, he usually had to do it himself.

Then one day, the receptionist, Emily, quit in a huff, frustrated by the amount of work that he was demanding of her. Edward was left with a desk full of papers and a telephone that wouldn't stop ringing.

Clueless about the work Emily had done, Edward was overwhelmed by having to pick up the pieces of a job that he didn't understand. His world turned upside down. He felt like a stranger in his own practice.

Why had he been such a fool? Why hadn't he taken the time to learn what Emily did in the office? Why had he waited until now?

Ever the trouper, Edward plowed into Emily's job with everything he could muster. What he found shocked him. Emily's work space was a disaster area! Her desk drawers were a jumble of papers, coins, pens, pencils, erasers, rubber bands, envelopes, business cards, and candy.

"What was she thinking?" Edward raged.

When he got home that night, even later than usual, he got into a shouting match with Abigail. He settled it by storming out of the house to get a drink. Didn't anybody understand him? Didn't anybody care what he was going through? Was there just no justice in the world?

He returned home only when he was sure that Abigail was asleep. As he walked by the computer, he noticed an unfinished e-mail up on the screen. One phrase practically leapt off the page: "Do you know of any good divorce lawyers in the area? I'd prefer not to use a former colleague of Edward's."

The e-mail was from his wife to her sister.

That night Edward slept on the couch. He left early in the morning before anyone was awake. For perhaps the first time in all his years as an attorney, he was in no mood for questions or arguments.

When Edward got to his office the next morning, he immediately headed for the liquor cabinet beside the desk . . . and you can imagine how the situation goes from here.

What lessons can we draw from Edward and Abigail's story? As I've already emphatically said, every business is a family business. Every business profoundly touches every family member, even those not working in the business. Every business either gives to the family or takes from the family, just as individual family members do.

If the business takes more than it gives, the family is always the first to pay the price.

In order for Edward to free himself from the prison he created, he would first have to admit his vulnerability. He would have to confess to himself and his family that he really doesn't know enough about his own practice and how to grow it.

Edward tried to do it all himself. Had he succeeded, had the practice supported his family in the style he imagined, he would have burst with pride. Instead, Edward unwittingly isolated himself, thereby achieving the exact opposite of what he sought.

He destroyed his life—and his family's life along with it.

Repeat after me: *Every business is a family business.*

Are you like Edward? I believe that all attorneys share a common soul with him. You must learn that a business is only a business. It is not your life. But it is also true that your business can have a profoundly negative impact on your life unless you learn how to do it differently than most attorneys do it, that is, differently than Edward did it.

Edward's legal practice could have served his and his family's life. But for that to happen, he would have had to learn how to master his practice in a way that was completely foreign to him.

Instead, Edward's practice consumed him. Lacking a true understanding of the essential strategic thinking that would have allowed him to create something unique, Edward and his family were doomed before he even opened his doors.

This book contains the secrets that Edward should have known. By applying the principles we'll discuss here, you can avoid a similar fate.

Let's start with the subject of *money*. But, before we do, let's listen to the lawyer's view about the story I just told you. Let's talk about the story of you and yours by Robert and Sandy.

www.michaelegerber.com/attorney

CHAPTER

2

The Story of You and Yours

Robert Armstrong
Sanford M. Fisch

Happiness resides not in possessions and not in gold;
The feeling of happiness dwells in the soul.

—Democritus

When we graduated from law school, we had a clear vision of what our future would be. We didn't need to worry about all the tedious (and often boring) aspects of running a business because let's face it—the rules for attorneys are different . . . aren't they?

After all, we practice a noble and revered profession. We've spent years learning our craft, taking difficult exams, and then, with much pomp and ceremony, we are granted the honor to pursue the lofty goal of practicing law. Let someone else worry about "business management" . . . we're "attorneys," for crying out loud.

And that's the first mistake most aspiring attorneys make.

We assume that we are immune from the heartaches and headaches that come with running a regular business. Yet after a short time, the harsh reality of the real world takes its toll just as it does with every other commercial enterprise. The most unfortunate part of this story is that we were never given the chance to learn what it means to actually practice law as a business. Quite the contrary—a new attorney is better equipped to file a brief with God than to be able to file papers at the courthouse, because that's what law schools teach.

As Professor Charles Kingsfield said in the 1973 movie, *The Paper Chase*:

> The study of law is something new and unfamiliar to most of you, unlike any other schooling you have ever known before. You teach yourselves the law, but I train your minds. You come in here with a skull full of mush and, if you survive, you'll leave thinking like a lawyer.

Obviously, we survived and Professor Kingsfield was right. . . . We came out thinking like lawyers. Too bad we didn't acquire a knack for business as well while we were there.

Ask any lawyer and he or she will agree: We're taught to be appellate judges, not practicing lawyers.

But in reality, we experience the same struggles you'd expect in any other business: attracting qualified and paying clients, delivering superior work, managing staff, and having a balanced life. In fact, we may struggle even more, because we never saw it as part of the deal.

Unfortunately, these struggles are manifesting into alarming statistics. A comprehensive study of attorneys found that of those in practice between 2 and 20 years, the rate of alcoholism was at 18%, but for those practicing more than 20 years, the rate spiked to an astonishing 25%. The study also found that severe depression was generally linked to prolonged and abusive drinking (GAH Benjamin, EJ Darling, B Sales, *International Journal of Law and Psychiatry*, 1990).

And while there are no definitive statistics, much anecdotal evidence suggests that the divorce rate among the legal and medical professions greatly exceeds the national average. But perhaps the most amazing fact of all is that practicing attorneys are willing to put up with the consequences of this mind-numbing stress, and they'll do it all for a median annual income of around $100,000. Those who own their own firms make even less (Bureau of Labor Statistics, *Occupational Outlook Handbook*, 2008–2009 edition).

This mass discontent with the profession was accidentally brought into focus many years ago by the California Bar Association. The Association used to publish a monthly poll in their official magazine that was delivered to every lawyer in the state. Sometimes the poll was about a technical issue, and other times about practice management. But one month, lawyers were asked whether they would recommend the practice of law to a family member or friend. The results were overwhelmingly negative. It caught everyone by surprise, but there it was—the great majority of the practicing lawyers in California, as we're sure is the case in every other state, could not, in good conscience, recommend their noble profession to those they loved.

Which brings us to the question at hand: Now that we've acknowledged all the shortcomings of our profession, what are we going to do about it?

We may have come from different places and different circumstances, but we've all arrived at the same place: We're attorneys trying to turn the practice of law into a successful business. We're struggling with long hours and late nights. We take files home and spend our weekends working instead of enjoying our families. We face the unreasonable demands of courts and clients, while files pile up on our desks and we do all of this for fees that are promised but often never paid.

And if this weren't bad enough, we get to watch as our dream of practicing law becomes a nightmare career path. The thing we once felt most passionately about slowly transforms into something we actually loathe. How did that happen? And what's worse, this growing gap between the life we imagined and the gritty reality we're facing is being played out around the country in rural locales and big cities alike.

Truth be told, most practitioners we've met over the years have created nothing more than a job, and not a very enjoyable one at that. You either work for someone else or you set up your own firm, in which case, as Michael likes to say, "You're working for a lunatic."

Yet regardless of where you started or where you are now, all of you created a family business. Yes, a family business, even though your family may not physically work there. Michael Gerber is right when he observes that it's impossible to keep your family insulated from the stress of the practice, no matter how hard you try.

We know firsthand the pressures associated with being a lawyer. And we also know those responsibilities are not easily left at the office. As attorneys, we are in command of many of the most important events in our clients' lives, and to clients, their case is always the most important matter in the office. Criminal matters might appear to be the most urgent, but clients left disabled by a defective product or facing financial ruin because their company's product was contaminated obviously carry some importance too. Add to that accidents, contracts, and custody suits, and it's easy to see that no single case can truly "outweigh" another.

And what's more, you're in charge of them all.

Nothing can be overlooked. Preparation can be endless. And because the very nature of our profession is built on conflict resolution, there's no such thing as having an "off day."

Let's face it, we're expected to go "all out" every time. That's just what an attorney does.

With all these pressing demands and deadlines, managing your time and energy needs to be your top priority. But therein lies the rub: How can you manage your time when it's spent managing everything else?

Interestingly, where you spent your time when you started practicing versus where you spend your time now is a revealing study. We've found that most began by seeking any business that would pay the bills. Success meant money, more clients, and more responsibility. As things became busy, of course, more staff was needed to meet the demands of the practice. More staff meant more payroll, so more business was needed to generate the money to meet that payroll, and more management was needed to oversee the staff.

Before you knew it, your time was being spent on things you never imagined and for which you had little aptitude or passion. You essentially went from the young lawyer eagerly waiting for the phone to ring to the experienced attorney cringing at the ringing phone because he knows too well that it brings nothing but problems.

After practicing law for decades and mentoring hundreds of lawyers, we know all too well what can rob you of your time on any given day. And this is time you can never recover. We also know what the day-to-day challenges are in the practice of law, and we understand how the demands of this profession can affect your daily life, your relationships, and your health.

So how did it happen? And more importantly, how do we stop it from continuing? There is hope for you, just as there is for all smart businesspeople who embrace the E-Myth way. Read on and discover how to take back your practice and your life.

www.michaelegerber.com/attorney

On the Subject of Money

Michael E. Gerber

Why is there so much month left at the end of the money?
—Anonymous

Had Edward and Abigail first considered the subject of *money* as we will here, their lives could have been radically different.

Money is on the tip of every attorney's tongue, on the edge (or at the very center) of every attorney's thoughts, intruding on every part of an attorney's life.

With money consuming so much energy, why do so few attorneys handle it well? Why was Edward, like so many attorneys, willing to entrust his financial affairs to a relative stranger? Why is money scarce for most attorneys? Why is there less money than expected? And yet the demand for money is *always* greater than anticipated.

What is it about money that is so elusive, so complicated, so difficult to control? Why is it that every attorney I've ever met hates to deal with the subject of money? Why are they almost always too late in facing money problems? And why are they constantly obsessed with the desire for more of it?

Money—you can't live with it and you can't live without it. But you better understand it and get your people to understand it. Because until you do, money problems will gnaw at your practice . . . and destroy what peace of mind you possess.

You don't need an accountant or financial planner to do the work I'm proposing. You simply need to prod your people to relate to money very personally. From senior partner to paralegal, everyone in your firm should understand the financial impact of what they do every day in relationship to the profit and loss of the practice.

And so you must teach your people to think like owners, not like paralegals or law clerks or temp workers. You must teach them to operate like personal profit centers, with a sense of how their work fits in with the practice as a whole.

You must involve everyone in the practice with the topic of money—how it works, where it goes, how much is left, and how much everybody gets at the end of the day. You also must teach them about the four kinds of money created by the practice.

The Four Kinds of Money

In the context of owning, operating, developing, and exiting from a legal practice, money can be split into four distinct but highly integrated categories:

1. Income
2. Profit
3. Flow
4. Equity

Failure to distinguish how the four kinds of money play out in your practice is a surefire recipe for disaster.

Important Note: Do not talk to your accountants or book-keepers about what follows; it will only confuse them and you. The information comes from the real-life experiences of thousands of small business owners, attorneys included, most of whom were hopelessly confused about money when I met them. Once they understood and accepted the following principles, they developed a clarity about money that could only be called enlightened. Your accountants and bookkeepers may be just as confused about money issues as your co-workers in your firm; if this is so, it wouldn't surprise me in the least.

The First Kind of Money: Income

Income is the money that attorneys are paid by their practice for doing their job *in* the practice. It's what they get paid for going to work every day.

Clearly, if attorneys didn't do their job, others would have to, and *they* would be paid the money the practice currently pays the attorneys. Income, then, has nothing to do with *ownership*. Income is solely the province of *employee-ship*.

That's why to the attorney-as-*employee*, income is the most important form that money can take. To the attorney-as-*owner*, however, it is the least important form that money can take.

Most important; least important. Do you see the conflict? The conflict between the attorney-as-employee and the attorney-as-owner?

We'll deal with this conflict later. For now, just know that it is potentially the most paralyzing conflict in an attorney's life.

Resolving this conflict will set you free!

The Second Kind of Money: Profit

Profit is what's left over after a legal practice has done its job effectively and efficiently. If there is no profit, the practice is doing something wrong.

However, just because the practice shows a profit does not mean that it is necessarily doing all the right things in the right way. Instead, it just means that something was done right during or preceding the period in which the profit was earned.

The important issue here is whether the profit was intentional or accidental. If it happened by accident (which is the case with most profit in law firms), don't take credit for it. You'll live to regret your impertinence.

If the profit occurred intentionally, take all the credit you want. You've earned it. Because profit created intentionally, rather than by accident, is replicable—again and again. And your practice's ability to repeat its performance is the most critical ability it can have.

As you'll soon see, the value of money is a function of your practice's ability to produce it in predictable amounts at an above-average return on investment.

Profit can be understood only in the context of your practice's purpose, as opposed to *your* purpose as an attorney. Profit, then, fuels the forward motion of the practice that produces it. This is accomplished in four ways:

1. Profit is *investment capital* that feeds and supports growth.
2. Profit is *bonus capital* that rewards people for exceptional work.
3. Profit is *operating capital* that shores up money shortfalls.
4. Profit is *return-on-investment* capital that rewards you, the attorney-owner, for taking risks.

Without profit, a legal practice cannot subsist, much less grow. Profit is the fuel of progress.

If a practice misuses or abuses profit, however, the penalty is much like having no profit at all. Imagine the plight of an attorney who has way too much return-on-investment capital and not enough investment capital, bonus capital, and operating capital. Can you see the imbalance this creates?

The Third Kind of Money: Flow

Flow is what money *does* in a legal practice, as opposed to what money *is*. Whether the practice is large or small, money tends to move erratically through it, much like a pinball. One minute it's there; the next minute it's not.

Flow can be even more critical to a practice's survival than profit, because a practice can produce a profit and still be short of money. Has this ever happened to you? It's called profit on paper rather than in fact.

No matter how large your practice, if the money isn't there when it's needed, you're threatened—regardless of how much profit you've made. You can borrow it, of course. But money acquired in dire circumstances is almost always the most expensive kind of money you can get.

Knowing where the money is and where it will be when you need it is a critically important task of both the attorney-as-employee and the attorney-as-owner.

Generally, two issues and two issues alone doom law firms: short-term cash flow problems and long-term cash flow problems. Otherwise, you have little to worry about.

Rules of Flow

You will learn no lesson more important than the huge impact that flow can have on the health and survival of your legal practice, let alone your business or enterprise. The following two rules will help you understand why this subject is so critical.

The First Rule of Flow states that your income statement is static, while flow is dynamic.

Your income statement is a snapshot, while the flow is a moving picture. So, while your income statement is an excellent tool for analyzing your practice *after* the fact, it's a poor tool for managing it in the heat of the moment.

Your income statement tells you (1) how much money you're spending and where, and (2) how much money you're receiving and from where.

Flow gives you the same information as the income statement, plus it tells you *when* you're spending and receiving money. In other words, flow is an income statement moving through time. And that is the key to understanding flow. It is about management in real time. How much is coming in? How much is going out? You'd like to know this daily, or even by the hour if possible. Never by the week or month.

You must be able to forecast flow. You must have a flow plan that helps you gain a clear vision of the money that's out there next month and the month after that. You must also pinpoint what your needs will be in the future.

Ultimately, however, when it comes to flow, the action is always in the moment. It's about now!

Unfortunately, few attorneys pay any attention to flow until it dries up completely and slow pay becomes no pay. They are oblivious to this kind of detail until, say, clients announce that they won't pay for this or that. That gets an attorney's attention because the expenses keep on coming.

When it comes to flow, most attorneys are flying by the proverbial seat of their pants. No matter how many people you hire to take care of your money, until you change the way you think about it, you will always be out of luck. No one can do this for you.

Managing flow takes attention to detail. But when flow is managed, your life takes on an incredible sheen. You're in charge! You're swimming with the current, not against it.

The Second Rule of Flow states that money seldom moves as you expect it to.

But you do have the power to change that, provided you understand the two primary sources of money as it comes in and goes out of your legal practice.

The truth is, the more control you have over the *source* of money, the more control you have over its flow. The sources of money are both inside and outside of your practice.

Money comes from *outside* your practice in the form of receivables, investments, and loans.

Money comes from *inside* your practice in the form of payables, taxes, capital investments, and payroll. These are the costs associated with attracting clients, delivering your services, operations, and so forth.

Few attorneys see the money going *out* of their practice as a source of money, but it is.

When considering how to spend money in your practice, you can save—and therefore make—money in three ways:

1. Do it more effectively.
2. Do it more efficiently.
3. Stop doing it altogether.

By identifying the money sources inside and outside of your practice, and then applying these methods, you will be immeasurably better at controlling the flow in your practice. But what are these sources? They include how you:

- Manage your services
- Compensate your people
- Plan people's use of time
- Determine the direct cost of your services
- Increase the time you spend seeing clients
- Manage your work
- Collect receivables

And countless more. In fact, every task performed in your practice (and ones you haven't yet learned how to perform) can be done more efficiently and effectively, dramatically reducing the cost of doing business. In the process, you will create more income, produce more profit, and balance the flow.

The Fourth Kind of Money: Equity

Sadly, few attorneys fully appreciate the value of equity in their legal practice. Yet, equity is the second most valuable asset any attorney will ever possess. (The first most valuable asset is, of course, your life. More on that later.)

Equity is the financial value placed on your practice by a prospective buyer of your practice.

Thus, your *practice* is your most important product, not your services, because your practice has the power to set you free. That's right. Once you sell your practice—providing you get what you want for it—you're free!

Of course, to enhance your equity, to increase your practice's value, you have to build it right. You have to build a practice that works. A practice that can become a true business and a business that can become a true enterprise. A practice/business/enterprise that can produce income, profit, flow, and equity better than any other attorney's practice/business/enterprise can.

To accomplish that, your practice must be designed so that it can do what it does systematically and predictably, every single time.

For the moment, don't let your technician's mind spoil this concept. The sale of a legal practice is a little different than the sale of other businesses, but what you'll be selling are the systems and the way of doing business which has more value than selling the clients themselves.

The Story of McDonald's

Let me tell you the most unlikely story anyone has ever told you about the successful building of a legal practice, business, and enterprise. Let me tell you the story of Ray Kroc.

You might be thinking, "What on earth does a hamburger stand have to do with my practice? I'm not in the hamburger business; I'm an attorney."

Yes, you are. But by practicing law as you have been taught, you've abandoned any chance to expand your reach, to touch more clients, and to improve legal services the way they must be improved if the practice of law—and your life—is going to be transformed.

In Ray Kroc's story lies the answer.

Ray Kroc called his first McDonald's restaurant "a little money machine." That's why thousands of franchises bought it. And the reason it worked? Ray Kroc demanded consistency, so that a hamburger in Philadelphia would be an advertisement for one in Peoria. In fact, no matter where you bought a McDonald's hamburger in the 1950s, the meat patty was guaranteed to weigh exactly 1.6 ounces, with a diameter of $3\frac{5}{8}$ inches. It was in the McDonald's handbook.

Did Ray Kroc succeed? You know he did! And so can you, once you understand his methods. Consider just one part of Ray Kroc's story.

In 1954, Ray Kroc made his living selling the five-spindle Multimixer milkshake machine. He heard about a hamburger stand in San Bernardino, California, which had eight of his machines in operation, meaning it could make 40 shakes simultaneously. That he had to see.

Kroc flew from Chicago to Los Angeles and then drove 60 miles to San Bernardino. As he sat in his car outside Mac and Dick McDonald's restaurant, he watched as lunch customers lined up for bags of hamburgers.

In a revealing moment, Kroc approached a strawberry blonde in a yellow convertible. As he later described it, "It was not her sex appeal but the obvious relish with which she devoured the hamburger that made my pulse begin to hammer with excitement."

Passion.

In fact, it was the french fry that truly captured his heart. Before the 1950s, it was almost impossible to buy fries of consistent quality. Ray Kroc changed all that. "The french fry," he once wrote, "would become almost sacrosanct for me, its preparation a ritual to be followed religiously."

Passion and preparation.

The potatoes had to be just so—top-quality Idaho russets, 8 ounces apiece, deep-fried to a golden brown, and salted with a shaker that, as Kroc put it, kept going "like a Salvation Army girl's tambourine."

As Kroc soon learned, potatoes too high in water content—and even top-quality Idaho russets varied greatly in water content—will come out soggy when fried. And so Kroc sent out teams of workers, armed with hydrometers, to make sure all his suppliers were producing potatoes in the optimal solids range of 20 to 23%.

Preparation and passion. Passion and preparation. Look those words up in the dictionary, and you'll see Ray Kroc's picture. Can you envision your picture there?

Do you understand what Ray Kroc did? Do you see why he was able to sell thousands of franchises? Kroc knew the true value of equity, and, unlike Edward from our story, Kroc went to work *on* his business rather than *in* his business. He knew the hamburger wasn't his product—McDonald's was!

So what does *your* legal practice need to do to become a little money machine? What is the passion that will drive you to build a practice that works—a turnkey system like Ray Kroc's?

Equity and the Turnkey System

What's a turnkey system? And why is it so valuable to you? To better understand it, let's look at another example of a turnkey system that worked to perfection: the recordings of Frank Sinatra.

Frank Sinatra's records were to him as McDonald's restaurants were to Ray Kroc. They were part of a turnkey system that allowed Sinatra to sing to millions of people without having to be there himself.

Sinatra's recordings were a dependable turnkey system that worked predictably, systematically, automatically, and effortlessly to produce the same results every single time—no matter where they were played, and no matter who was listening.

Regardless of where Frank Sinatra was, his records just kept on producing income, profit, flow, and equity, over and over . . . and still do! Sinatra needed only to produce the prototype recording and the system did the rest.

Kroc's McDonald's is another prototypical turnkey solution, addressing everything McDonald's needs to do in a basic, systematic way so that anyone properly trained by McDonald's can successfully reproduce the same results.

And this is where you'll realize your equity opportunity: in the way your practice does business; in the way your practice systematically does what you intend it to do; and in the development of your turnkey system—a system that works even in the hands of ordinary people (and attorneys less experienced than you) to produce extraordinary results.

Remember:

- If you want to build vast equity in your practice, then go to work *on* your practice, building it into a business that works every single time.

- Go to work *on* your practice to build a totally integrated turnkey system that delivers exactly what you promised every single time.

- Go to work *on* your practice to package it and make it stand out from the legal practices you see everywhere else.

Here is the most important idea you will ever hear about your practice and what it can potentially provide for you:

The value of your equity is directly proportional to how well your practice works. And how well your practice works is directly proportional to the effectiveness of the systems you have put into place upon which the operation of your practice depends.

Whether money takes the form of income, profit, flow, or equity, the amount of it—and how much of it stays with you—invariably boils down to this. Money, happiness, life—it all depends on how well your practice works, not on your people, not on you, but on the system.

Your practice holds the secret to more money. Are you ready to learn how to find it?

Earlier in this chapter, I alerted you to the inevitable conflict between the attorney-as-employee and the attorney-as-owner. It's a battle between the part of you working *in* the practice and the part of you working *on* the practice. Between the part of you working for income and the part of you working for equity.

Here's how to resolve this conflict:

1. Be honest with yourself about whether you're filling *employee* shoes or *owner* shoes.

2. As your practice's key employee, determine the most effective way to do the job you're doing, *and then document that job.*

3. Once you've documented the job, create a strategy for replacing yourself with someone else (another attorney, or, even better, a paralegal) who will then use your documented system exactly as you do.

4. Have your new employees manage the newly delegated system. Improve the system by quantifying its effectiveness over time.

5. Repeat this process throughout your practice wherever you catch yourself acting as employee rather than owner.

6. Learn to distinguish between ownership work and employee-ship work every step of the way.

Master these methods, understand the differences among the four kinds of money, develop an interest in how money works in your practice, and then watch it flow in!

Now let's take another step in our strategic thinking process. Let's look at the subject of *planning*. But, first, let's listen to what Robert and Sandy have to say about money.

www.michaelegerber.com/attorney

Your Money or Your Life?

Robert Armstrong
Sanford M. Fisch

There is only one success—to be able to spend your life in your own way.

—Christopher Morley

What is it about money that drives us to insanity? Somewhere along the way, we got the notion that money was the key to happiness and although publicly we might deny that we live by such an absurd and shallow concept, our actions say otherwise.

Every day, we meet seemingly educated and intelligent people who still behave as if their happiness level is directly tied to the number of zeros in their bank account. And ironically, the harder and longer they work, the less they seem to have of either. But rather than stop the insanity and try a new approach, these intelligent, educated people find ways to devote even more hours to the alchemic art of turning money into happiness.

So, does this mean that you have to choose between being happy and making some real dough? Are we suggesting that you can't have both? Absolutely not! In fact, we're all for prosperity and "living the good life" and we applaud your determination to create a comfortable and financially secure existence for you and yours.

It's not the dream that we're questioning here. . . . It's the approach that needs some work, and if there's one thing you take away from this book, let it be this: Money alone will not give you the life you're looking for—only you can do that. What's more, to get to that life you're seeking, you have to give up the idea that you are what you do.

After coaching attorneys for many years, we've noticed that the most difficult perspective for them to grasp is that they have a business or practice that is separate from themselves. The notion that they are forever destined to trade time for dollars is deeply, and sometimes hopelessly, ingrained. Lawyers are convinced that if they just get more cases and work longer hours all their money problems will be over.

But what they fail to realize is that even if they do generate more cash flow, they are sacrificing something worth far more—themselves. And that isn't a recipe for success, but rather one that guarantees burnout and disaster.

A huge breakthrough occurs when they realize they can create a business that will leverage their time and the revenue of the firm. However, this new awareness of "lawyer as entrepreneur" has to be reinforced often so they don't inevitably slip back into the "lawyer as employee" mind-set. Remember, the underlying purpose of this book is for you to take stock of your practice and be honest about whether you can separate your duties as an owner from the actual work you do. Just as Ray Kroc realized that his product wasn't making hamburgers, but rather, the business that made the hamburgers, all attorneys who come to think of the law practice itself as the real product of their efforts are on their way to a better, more rewarding life. You then will start to see your practice as a separate thing that you can mold, engineer, tinker with, and redesign any way you want, like an architect looking at the model of the structure she plans to build. Can you do that? Can you step back and see the parts of your law practice as components that can be optimized and systematized?

If not, then all the strategies we're going to lay out for you in this book will make no sense. However, once you grasp the fundamental distinction between your work as an employee and your responsibility as an owner—you have entered the exciting world of designer, builder, architect, and creator of your business life. It's important to note that the skills of a business owner are not the same as those of a first-class lawyer. Just because you're a great legal technician doesn't mean you know what it takes to run a business that provides legal services. Competency in business doesn't come naturally, and if these concepts are new, you can't really be blamed. Law schools, traditionally, have not focused on the business of law. They are in the technician business, teaching students how to think like lawyers and solve legal issues. Recently some progressive schools have begun to address this obvious shortcoming in the typical law school curriculum. However, that does precious little for existing practitioners slugging it out in the trenches, trying to meet payroll today and create a better life for their families. If you're willing to suspend all your beliefs about what it takes to build a successful law firm, this book will give you a new track to run on. It will be a chance to reorganize your thoughts and right the ship before it sinks.

Once you're clear about your vision of your law firm as a business, commit it to writing and passionately communicate it to everyone in the practice, from the receptionist, to the paralegals, to the bookkeeper, to the other attorneys, and even to your family if you hope to get support for this new way of serving clients and earning a living. Clear, effective communication with your staff is critical for your new venture. Because your business will be run in large part by employees, it's imperative they all understand the big picture, and make no mistake about it, the big picture is about money, finances, profitability, paychecks, and bonuses—yes, bonuses!

The first step we generally recommend to our coaching clients is to know their number. What that means is what specific monetary goal do you have for your business? Surprisingly, most attorneys have never given this any thought. Is it $1,000,000 in your pocket on an annual basis? $500,000? $5,000,000? Whatever amount you realistically think your practice is capable of producing, write it down and we'll work backwards to make that tantalizing number real. What we really want to know is what amount of revenue must your firm generate every day to make your dream number a reality. No vague yearly, monthly, or weekly number to start, but a revenue goal that you can see on a daily basis. When you go home at night, you've either hit your number or you've missed it and everyone in the firm plays the game.

Getting to your daily number is just a formula with a few moving parts. It will form the single-minded goal for your entire practice team, so don't skip over this part. It will create your dream practice and give you incredible focus. Here's how you create your daily number.

First, we know there are 52 weeks in a year, but let's create a life where you have four weeks of vacation. That knocks it down to 48 weeks. We all know that very little gets done in the last couple of weeks before Christmas, so let's take off another couple of weeks there, which brings us to 46 weeks. Forty-six weeks equal 322 days, but we can't forget national holidays. The United States has 11 national holidays, and let's assume you take all of those off as well (322 − 11 = 311). Finally, you don't want to be working on the weekends, so there goes another 92 days (46 weekends), which gives you a working year of about 219 days.

To round out this exercise, take your firm's dream revenue number—let's say it's $1,000,000—and divide it by 219 days. That should give you a daily revenue number of $4,566. If your expenses run at 50% of gross, that will net you $500,000 in your pocket before taxes. Obviously you can play with whatever numbers you want, but we think you get the idea. Now write your number down and let everyone know that for this firm to be successful as a business, every day the crew must bring in $4,566.

Once your team buys into this game, the possibilities are endless. Mini-celebrations can be arranged weekly, monthly, or quarterly for hitting the goals. Let them know that bonuses are dependent on those numbers, so it's no longer a mystery how money is distributed. Believe this: Once you frame your number properly, everyone will jump on board. Client fees will magically get collected. Vendors will have every bill scrutinized from the receptionist through the senior partner. Requests for frivolous expenditures will stop, and more importantly, each employee will start paying attention to the productivity of other staff members. If some slack off, others will be there to remind them that they're messing with their bonuses. Over the years, we've seen it work miracles in a firm's profitability and sense of mission.

The four factors of money that Michael Gerber detailed are critically important for law firms to understand. We think you'll agree that income, profit, flow, and equity cover a lot of ground. Before you picked up this book, you probably measured your compensation by combining income and profit. In other words, whatever is left over after paying everyone else is yours to keep. Understanding what Michael calls *flow* requires that you actually analyze the ebb and flow of money through your practice. Depending on your type of practice, you may have noticed that it has a rhythm of its own. Contingency fee lawyers see wild fluctuations in revenue and expenses. Lawyers billing on an hourly basis often see predictable patterns. Whatever the variations, you need a strategy to ensure that there are always funds available.

Regardless of the type of practice, we recommend that you secure an adequate line of credit (LOC) to withstand the flow variances and smooth out the accounts receivable from the accounts payable. This is an extremely savvy business practice, whether you think you need it or not. We've seen the devastating impact to law practices when new credit is not available, and in truth, the best time to ask for an LOC is when you don't need the money. That's when institutions are more likely to say yes because it's a low-risk business for them.

So, regardless of whether you're starting a practice or enhancing your current business, now is the time to get your "unneeded" LOC. To navigate credit issues, we recommend that you establish at least one solid relationship with a local banker. It's the personal relation-ship that makes all the difference. Take the time to seek one out and candidly explain the kind of practice you have and your credit needs. In tough times, it will be that person who takes up your cause to the nameless committees that make the decisions.

Now, these trusted bankers sometimes move from institution to institution as they seek to advance their careers, and generally, we recommend that you move with them. That's why it's so important to choose your banker wisely. In shaky times, their credit life lines may mean the difference between prosperity and bankruptcy, so don't overlook the importance of this relationship.

Another "money" relationship you will want to foster is a strong bond with a good certified public accountant (CPA) or experienced bookkeeper. Most small law firms and solo practitioners we've dealt with over the years have tried to skimp on this relationship. In fact, many lawyers are running their practices out of their checkbooks or a personal copy of Quicken. But if you're committed to having a business, you need to have instant control and access to your numbers. In fact, your numbers tell a story about your firm. It's unbiased, unsentimental, and devoid of wishful thinking. Every law firm should have a strong relationship with an accountant who knows your story and can interpret it for you.

No later than the tenth day of every month, you should schedule a meeting, either in person or by phone, with your "numbers person" to let you know the truth about the prior month. It's the perfect chance for you to work on your business to make sure it's profitable and has liquidity. You'll also want to make sure equity is accumu-lating. The accountant should go over the monthly income state-ment and balance sheet and point out any patterns, good or bad. It's also a chance to review your expenses to make sure they're in check.

To zero in on particular numbers, a good accountant can use various benchmarks or ratios to judge the health of your practice. Over the years, we've created several for estate planning attorneys that help them pinpoint the metrics that count. The ratios may be different among different types of practices, but taking the time to identify those numbers will pay huge dividends down the road. If a particular month shows that these ratios are out of whack, red flags go up and you can take corrective action. The Internal Revenue Service (IRS) has even taken national surveys to help you sort out some often-used ratios for various parts of your business. Common size ratios, for example, express each category from your balance sheet as a percentage of your total assets and liabilities. You can do the same with the income statement and calculate the percentage of each income item to your total sales. Your current ratio divides the current assets by your current liabilities to show the financial health of the enterprise.

Want to know whether you're overstaffed? The revenue per employee ratio can help you do just that. You may end up using all of these ratios or just a select few—your accountant can tailor the ones that are most meaningful for your firm.

And what will all the ratios do for you? Well, wouldn't it be helpful to know what percentage of your revenue should be devoted to marketing or rent or salaries? Would you like to know the cost of a client acquisition? How about a healthy ratio for owner's compensation? Without these numbers on a monthly basis, you're flying blind.

The last Gerber factor about money is equity. Most attorneys don't think about equity because, as we've said before, they don't think about their law practice as a business. Consequently, they never consider the natural conclusion of an enterprise, that is, the profitable exit or the sale of the practice. In fact, most attorneys are under the mistaken belief that ethical rules prohibit the sale of a practice. While in concept that may be true in many jurisdictions, our philosophy has always been that the value of your practice is in your systems, and those can be sold for a handsome sum. We'll talk more about that later but starting now, we urge you to be constantly aware of your practice's equity. The very essence of a business is to kick out current income and consistently build equity so there will be a pot of money down the road when it's time for you to go.

For now, take time to examine the "money issues" in your current practice and see how you stack up with the four factors. Then envision how you could take all four money factors into account going forward in your practice. The gap between the way you used to think about money and how you now think about money will be closed as we move forward and begin the planning process.

www.michaelegerber.com/attorney

CHAPTER

5

On the Subject of Planning

Michael E. Gerber

*He who every morning plans the transaction of the day and follows out
that plan, carries a thread that will guide him through the maze of the
most busy life.*

*But where no plan is laid, where the disposal of time is surrendered
merely to the chance of incidence, chaos will soon reign.*

—Victor Hugo

Another obvious oversight revealed in Edward and Abigail's
story was the absence of true planning.

Every attorney starting his or her own practice must
have a plan. You shouldn't even begin to see clients without one.
But, like Edward, most attorneys do. In fact, rare is the attorney who
can or will provide a direct answer to any client's direct question. As
the old joke goes, "Why can't an attorney practice law if he breaks
his arm? Because he can't say, 'On the one hand . . . '"

It's no joke, however.

An attorney lacking a vision is simply someone who goes to work
every day. Someone who is just doing it, doing it, doing it. Busy, busy,

busy. Maybe making money, maybe not. Maybe getting something out of life, maybe not. Taking chances without really taking control.

The plan tells anyone who needs to know *how we do things here.* The plan defines the objective and the process by which you will attain it. The plan encourages you to organize tasks into functions, and then helps people grasp the logic of each of those functions. This in turn permits you to bring new employees up to speed quickly.

There are numerous books and seminars on the subject of Practice Management, but they focus on making you a better attorney. I want to teach you something else that you've never been taught before: how to be a manager and an entrepreneur. It has nothing to do with conventional practice management and everything to do with thinking like an entrepreneur.

The Planning Triangle

As we discussed in the Preface, every legal practice is a company, every legal business is a company, and every legal enterprise is a company. Yet the differences among the three are extraordinary. Although all three may offer legal services, how they do what they do is completely different.

The trouble with most companies owned by attorneys is that they are dependent on the attorney. That's because they're practices—the smallest, most limited form a company can take. Practices are formed around the technician, whether attorney or roofer.

You may choose in the beginning to form a practice, but you should understand its limitations. The company called a *practice* depends on the owner—that is, the attorney. The company called a *business* depends on other people plus a system by which that business does what it does. Once your practice becomes a business, you can replicate it, turning it into an *enterprise.*

Consider the example of Helen D. Hawthorne Law Offices. The clients don't come in asking for Ms. Hawthorne. Although she is one of the top attorneys around, Helen can only handle so many cases a day. Yet she wants to offer her high-quality services to more people in the community. If she has reliable systems in place—systems that any qualified technician can learn to use—she has created a business and it can be replicated. Helen can then go on to offer her services that—demand her guidance, not her presence—in a multitude of different settings. She can open dozens of legal companies, none of which need Helen Hawthorne herself, except in the role of entrepreneur.

Is your legal company going to be a practice, a business, or an enterprise? Planning is crucial to answering this all-important question. Whatever you choose to do must be communicated by your plan, which is really three interrelated plans in one. We call it the *planning triangle* (Figure 5.1), and it consists of the following:

- Business plan
- Practice plan
- Completion plan

FIGURE 5.1 Planning Triangle

The three plans form a triangle, with the business plan at the base, the practice plan in the center, and the completion plan at the apex. The business plan determines *who* you are (the business), the practice plan determines *what* you do (the specific focus of your legal practice), and the completion plan determines *how* you do it (the fulfillment process).

By looking at the planning triangle, we see that the three critical plans are interconnected. The connection among them is established by asking the following questions:

1. Who are we?
2. What do we do?
3. How do we do it?

   Who are we? is purely a strategic question.

   What do we do? is both a strategic and a tactical question.

   How do we do it? is both a strategic and a tactical question.

Strategic questions shape the vision and destiny of your business, of which your practice is only one essential component. Tactical questions turn that vision into reality. Thus, strategic questions provide the foundation for tactical questions, just as the base provides the foundation for the middle and apex of your planning triangle.

First ask: What do we do and how do we do it . . . *strategically?*
And then: What do we do and how do we do it . . . *practically?*

Let's look at how the three plans will help you develop your practice.

The Business Plan

Your business plan will determine what you choose to do in your legal practice and the way you choose to do it. Without a business plan, your practice can do little more than survive. And even that will take more than a little luck.

Without a business plan you're treading water in a deep pool with no shore in sight. You're working against the natural flow.

I'm not talking about the traditional business plan that is taught in business schools. No, this business plan reads like a story—the most important story you will ever tell.

Your business plan must clearly describe:

- The business you are creating
- The purpose it will serve
- The vision it will pursue
- The process through which you will turn that vision into a reality
- The way money will be used to realize your vision

Build your business plan with *business* language, not *practice* language (the language of the attorney, associate, paralegal, whomever). Make sure the plan focuses on matters of interest to your lenders and shareholders rather than just your technicians. It should rely on demographics and psychographics to tell you who buys and why; it should also include projections for return on investment and return on equity. Use it to detail both the market and the strategy through which you intend to become a leader in that market, not as an attorney but as a business enterprise.

The business plan, although absolutely essential, is only one of three critical plans that every attorney needs to create and implement. Now let's take a look at the practice plan.

The Practice Plan

The practice plan includes everything an attorney needs to know, have, and do, in order to deliver his or her promise to a client on time, every time. Every task should prompt you to ask three questions:

1. What do I need to know?
2. What do I need to have?
3. What do I need to do?

What Do I Need to Know?

What information do I need to satisfy my promise on time, every time, exactly as promised? In order to recognize what you need to know, you must understand the expectations and limitations of others, including your clients, partners, associates, paralegals, and other employees. Are you clear on those expectations? Don't make the mistake of assuming that you know. Instead, create a *need-to-know checklist* to make sure that you ask all the necessary questions.

A need-to-know checklist might look like this:

- What are the expectations of my clients?
- What are the expectations of my partners and associates?
- What are the expectations of my paralegals?
- What are the expectations of my staff?

What Do I Need to Have?

This question raises the issue of resources—namely, money, people, and time. If you don't have enough money to finance operations, how can you fulfill those expectations without creating cash flow problems? If you don't have enough trained people, what happens then? And if you don't have enough time to manage your practice, what happens when you can't be in two places at once?

Don't assume that you can get what you need when you need it. Most often, you can't. And even if you can get what you need at the last minute, you will pay dearly for it.

What Do I Need to Do?

The focus here is on actions to be started and finished. What do I need to do to fulfill the expectations of this client on time, every time, exactly as promised? To use a specific example: What exactly are the steps to perform for a client who is filing a civil lawsuit against a former employer in state court?

Your clients fall into distinct categories, and those categories make up your practice. The best legal practices will invariably focus on fewer and fewer categories, as the attorneys who own them discover the importance of doing one thing better than anyone else.

Answering the question, *What do I need to do?*, demands a series of action plans, including:

- The objective to be achieved
- The standards by which you will know that the objective has been achieved
- The benchmarks you need to reach in order for the objective to be achieved
- The function/person accountable for the completion of the benchmarks
- The budget for the completion of each benchmark
- The time by which each benchmark must be completed

Your action plans should become the foundation for the completion plans. And the reason you need completion plans is to assure that everything you do is not only realistic but can also be managed.

The Completion Plan

If the practice plan gives you results and provides you with standards, the completion plan tells you everything you need to know about every benchmark in the practice plan—that is, how you're going to fulfill client expectations on time, every time, as promised. In other words, how you're going to draft a pre-nup or educate a client on your state's probate laws.

The completion plan is essentially the operations manual, providing information about the details of doing tactical work. It is a guide to tell the people responsible for doing that work exactly how to do it.

Every completion plan becomes a part of the knowledge base of your business. No completion plan goes to waste. Every completion plan becomes a kind of textbook that explains to new employees or new associates joining your team how your practice operates in a way that distinguishes it from all other legal practices.

To return to an earlier example, the completion plan for making a Big Mac is explicitly described in the *McDonald's Operation Manual*, as is every completion plan needed to run a McDonald's business.

The completion plan for an attorney might include the step-by-step details of how to prepare an appellate brief—in contrast to how everyone else has learned to do it. Of course, anyone who works in law has learned how to prepare briefs. They've learned to do it the same way everyone else has learned to do it. But if you are going to stand out as unique in the minds of your clients, employees, and others, you must invent your own way of doing even ordinary things. You must constantly raise the questions: *How do we do it here? How should we do it here?*

The quality of your answers will determine how effectively you distinguish your practice from every other attorney's practice.

Benchmarks

You can measure the movement of your practice—from what it is today to what it will be in the future—using business benchmarks. These are the goals you want your business to achieve during its lifetime.

Your benchmarks should include the following:

- Financial benchmarks
- Emotional benchmarks (the impact your practice will have on everyone who comes into contact with it)
- Performance benchmarks
- Client benchmarks (Who are they? Why do they come to you? What will your practice give them that no one else will?)
- Employee benchmarks (How do you grow people? How do you find people who want to grow? How do you create a school in your practice that will teach your people skills they can't learn anywhere else?)

Your business benchmarks will reflect (1) the position that your practice will hold in the minds and hearts of your clients, employees, and investors, and (2) how you intend to make that position a reality through the systems you develop.

Your benchmarks will describe how your management team will take shape and what systems you will need to develop so that your managers, just like McDonald's managers, will be able to produce the results for which they will be held accountable.

Benefits of the Planning Triangle

By implementing the Planning Triangle, you will discover:

- What your practice will look, act, and feel like when it's fully evolved
- When that's going to happen
- How much money you will make

And much, much more.

These, then, are the primary purposes of the three critical plans: (1) to clarify precisely what needs to be done to get what the attorney wants from his or her practice and life, and (2) to define the specific steps by which it will happen.

First *this* must happen, then *that* must happen. One, two, three. By monitoring your progress, step by step, you can determine whether you're on the right track.

That's what planning is all about. It's about creating a standard—a yardstick—against which you will be able to measure your performance.

Failing to create such a standard is like throwing a straw into a hurricane. Who knows where that straw will land?

(To find out exactly what your three critical plans will look like when they're finished, go to www.michaelegerber.com/attorney and click on "The E-Myth Attorney.")

Have you taken the leap? Have you accepted that the word "business" and the word "practice" are not synonymous? That a practice relies on the attorney and a business relies on other people plus a system?

Many attorneys justify their evasion of their responsibility to run their practice as a business on the ground that to focus on "business" is somehow immoral or unethical for an attorney. They tell themselves that there is something impure, inelegant, or even unprofessional about thinking of their practice in business terms.

Because most attorneys are control freaks, 99% of today's legal companies are practices, not businesses.

The result, as a lawyer friend of mine says, is that "attorneys are spending all day stamping out fires when all around them the forest is ablaze. They're out of touch, and that attorney better take control of the practice before someone else does."

Because attorneys are never taught to think like businesspeople, legal professional is forever at war with businessperson. This is especially evident in large firms, where bureaucrats (businesspeople) often try to control attorneys (legal professionals). They usually end up treating each other as combatants. In fact, the single greatest reason that attorneys become entrepreneurs is to divorce such bureaucrats and to begin to reinvent the legal enterprise.

That's you. Now the divorce is over and a new love affair has begun. You're an attorney with a plan! Who wouldn't want to do business with such a person?

Now let's take the next step in our Strategic Odyssey and take a closer look at the subject of *management*. But, before we do, let's listen to what Robert and Sandy have to say about planning.

www.michaelegerber.com/attorney

CHAPTER
6

Plotting Your Course

Robert Armstrong
Sanford M. Fisch

Man first of all exists, encounters himself, surges up in the world—and defines himself afterwards.
—John Paul Sartre, *Existentialism Is Humanism*

After reading Michael's chapter on planning, you should feel pretty excited about this new shift in perspective and all the opportunities it brings. More likely however, you're probably just thinking, "Planning? Who has time to plan? I've got way too much to do already!"

Sound familiar?

But what Michael gave you in Chapter 5 is essentially a blueprint to transform your "practice" into a "business," and if you follow it, we can assure you that it works. It works so well, in fact, that we use it in our own business and teach it to the hundreds of clients we've personally coached over the years.

So, take note: This is what you've been waiting for.

Now, while we don't intend to reiterate Michael's comments here, it is important for us to highlight certain components of the planning process as well as add some key elements specifically for you, the attorney. So, we'll start with a baseline developed from firsthand experience and in our relationships with attorneys and their firms around the country, and then we'll go from there.

Ready?

Here it is: You do superior legal work but the practice has not matured into a profitable business and you feel frustrated and helpless to make your dreams come true. You are convinced that your daily schedule does not permit the time to think about "working on the business" because you have too many more urgent matters waiting on your desk every morning. Clients and meetings and court dates and busy work are just a few of the things that are keeping you from the all-important activity of strategic planning. And of course, let's not forget, you need to stay on top of the law, keep the documents you use in your practice up to date, monitor new emerging legal strategies, new court cases, and let's see . . . make sure your law firm is equipped with the latest technology. Have we missed anything?

You're expected to do all of this while making sure that you pay attention to staff, provide training when they need it, and schedule performance reviews in a timely manner. This long list of responsibilities has caused many to look at planning as a sort of academic exercise for those with nothing to do.

You, on the other hand, have to get back to work. Unfortunately, that means busy work, the "doing it, doing it, doing it" all day long, and for most attorneys, into the night and on weekends as well.

But in reality, ignoring the time to "sharpen the saw" and critically look at your practice as a business is the one thing that's preventing you from developing a predictably profitable enterprise.

We've found that regardless of how many pressing matters might be demanding your attention, real-world planning must be the engine that guides all your business decisions. The most important part of your day, your week, your month, and each and every year, is committing your vision to writing and then mapping out the steps to make it happen. This may not be an easy task, and it may go against your natural instinct to jump in and get things done, but you must set aside time for this strategic activity.

As Michael Gerber pointed out many years ago in his landmark book, *The E-Myth*, the primary purpose of your business is to serve your needs, to be a vehicle for your happiness and fulfillment. Unfortunately, this first principle has been turned on its head. Not long after new attorneys get into the groove of practicing, something amazing happens: The practice starts running them instead. Or as Emerson once wisely said, "[T]hings are in the saddle and ride mankind." In the case of far too many lawyers we meet, the practice has become the master and the owner's dream takes a back seat.

That's why we like the triangle structure detailed in Chapter 5 so much. This is a perfect model for attorneys, regardless of your practice area—you just need to set aside a couple of days of focused time to think about how it can work in your firm. Simply asking "Who are we? What do we do? How do we do it?" can often be all it takes to open the channels to a new way of thinking. Chances are that these fundamental questions have never been asked because the technician in you just jumped in and started practicing. Well, consider this book your "time-out" from all that frantic activity. It could very well be the savior of not only your business, but of your life as well. That is, of course, if you take the time to follow these recommendations and put them to use. Reading the words and understanding the concepts are not enough. You must take action to see the rewards.

So, let's start where Michael started in the planning process and tailor these plans to your firm.

Your Business Plan

Your plan should not be a dry academic piece, but a rich story about this business you've brought into existence. It's something much more than a means to put bread on the table. It has a purpose in the community and will impact shareholders, employees, vendors, and of course, clients. The business plan will be your firm's constitution, outlining your vision and how you plan to bring it into reality.

To get started, you'll want to calendar some time for a personal retreat to really explore your practice, its purpose, and how it fits with your original intention. We think your first exercise should be to honestly look at the specific area of law in which you are practicing, or in some cases, where you want to practice. We mention this core issue because we have seen so many attorneys who deeply hate their practice area. They got into their specific area in a variety of ways, none of which had anything to do with what they really wanted out of their legal career. Perhaps they had a job with a firm where someone was needed in the bankruptcy department and presto, you're a bankruptcy lawyer. Others got involved in litigation, no doubt attracted by the glamour and excitement of trial work, only to find a life filled with stress and conflict, occasionally punctuated by an actual trial.

But despite how you got there, we know that practicing in an area where you have no passion or joy is a recipe for unhappiness regardless of the money you make. So, set aside all those reasons and circumstances that have brought you to where you are now. Put all your cards on the table and invent the life you want. It's never too late, and who knows? You may fall in love with your practice choice all over again.

It may take some soul searching to come to grips with your feelings about your current practice area, but don't underestimate the importance of this journey. To be fulfilled, you must have a burning desire to go to work each day and build your practice. If that is not how you feel, you need to reconsider what you are doing. Over the years we have spoken to groups of attorneys around the country and we always focus on the wide field of opportunity within the law. We understand the significant investment and personal sacrifice just to have your license to practice, not to mention the additional effort invested in gaining expertise in a specific practice area.

But, if you don't have the passion for your practice, you should give serious consideration to exploring other options the law has to offer. Think about the advice you would give to a new attorney about choosing a specific area of law and then give yourself that same advice and follow it. The reality is that the same opportunity exists for every attorney, regardless of experience level or years in practice.

And the bottom line is that this is your life. It's your livelihood. This is where most of your waking hours will be spent, so it had better be exciting, it better be fun, and you better want to do it. If you don't feel passion for your work, then you're setting yourself up to fail because you'll be competing against others who truly believe in what they do. It's not enough to just climb the wall efficiently. You want to make sure you're climbing the right wall, too.

Once the decision about your practice area has been made, you'll see its significance and implications on many fronts. First, everything else becomes easier. Now, by "easier," we don't mean that everything just magically gets done. What we do mean is that your decision becomes the overriding principle in your business and allows you to say the most important word you'll ever say as you build your practice. That word is "no." You need to begin to say "no" to all the requests and opportunities that don't further your chosen path. As a business person, many opportunities will come your way. Many will sound amazingly attractive, and more often than not, they will promise a life better than what you've chosen, whether it's more money, less work, more prestige, or any other number of appealing scenarios.

But—and this is the hard part—you need to have the conviction in your business decision and the discipline to say "no" to everything that isn't part of your written plan. You see, all those other opportunities, favors, and requests might appear golden on the surface, but in truth, they do nothing but distract you from your mission, while wasting your energy and focus. We've found that those who truly succeed in creating a life they love pick a path and stick to it.

So, that's what you need to do as well. And when you say "no," you reinforce your conviction in your chosen path and your decision to pursue your goals. This kind of conviction gives you the confidence you need to build the business you want. Saying "no" to rogue opportunities also sends a message to others that you're serious about your plan.

It tells your staff, your vendors, your colleagues, and your prospects that you are committed to your practice and to the mission you've set forth. And if you think that's not important, think again. The best person to work on your pipes is a plumber, not an electrician. Likewise, the best person to diagnose an illness is a doctor, not a car salesman, and this same concept is true with attorneys as well.

If you want to be a bankruptcy attorney, then that's exactly what you should be. If you want to work in family law, then that's where you should put all your efforts. Pick your path and then stick with it. Your conviction will resonate throughout your practice.

Your Practice Plan

The next area of planning represents the snapshot of your firm. As Michael puts it, the "what we do" piece to the puzzle. This incorporates your revenue goals, the services your practice will provide, the markets it will target, the geographic areas it will reach, and, of course, the realistic time frame needed to accomplish all of these goals. Add to that the location of your office, the initial number of employees, and your anticipated staff growth, and you'll begin to see your practice plan take shape.

Want to really put this planning thing to work? Look forward and project when and how your business will grow. Anticipate what additional services that clients will need or want and, more importantly, be willing to pay for. Actually, this isn't as difficult as it might sound. You can learn quite a bit just by asking your existing clients. If the questions are properly framed, you'll be amazed at the quality of the feedback that your clients will provide.

After you have the "what" figured out, you can move on to the details of "how." That is, how can you tactically make it all happen?

Obviously, you'll need systems in place for a variety of things, including marketing, converting prospects to clients, and, of course, actually getting the work done. But don't assume that these systems are the same ones you remember from "way back when." In fact, don't even assume that the systems you have in place right now are actually the systems you need.

Doing business in the twenty-first century is a whole new ball game. The old traditional methods of partner announcements, golf outings, and the old Yellow Page advertisements have given way to a dizzying array of new marketing tools. Seminars, direct mail, e-mail, newspaper ads, web sites, billboards, and teleconferences are just a sampling of what's available, and that doesn't even touch on the world of social networking.

Marketing in the digital age includes new ways of reaching people—often called Web 2.0—and what's more, these methods are changing and expanding all the time. These new tools allow for interactive communication between the law firm and prospects, allowing the public to comment on your services and their experience with your firm. Some of the most recent popular Web 2.0 sites you might want to consider include LinkedIn, AVVO, Facebook, Twitter, Blogging, YouTube, Legal OnRamp, Martindale.com, and Lawyers.com.

And like we said, the playing field is constantly changing, so it's difficult to know which platforms will survive. But one thing is certain: It's impossible to ignore the strength and reach of these new tools. Your law firm should consider all of them as your marketing strategy takes shape.

Your Completion Plan

Of course, the heart of your business building process will revolve around establishing and documenting systems for every part of your practice. If you think this sounds like a tedious waste of time, then know this: This step—more than any other—will quickly transform a chaotic and inefficient practice into a real business with a life apart from the owners.

So, for every task, every job, and every function that is done in the firm on an even semi-regular basis, there should be a system. You should have a system for developing leads. A system for answering the phone. A system for greeting clients, for setting up the conference room, and for corresponding with clients and opposing counsel. You'll also need a system for filing documents, as well as a system for hiring new personnel, for giving performance reviews, and for letting a staff member go when his or her performance isn't meeting the expectations of your practice.

Are you getting the picture?

Whatever area you practice in, there should be a well-developed group of systems that details every area of that practice. If an employee leaves and a new one comes on board, they should be able to review an operations manual that not only outlines the company's policies and culture, but also documents the proper way to perform his or her job as well as the way that performance will be measured. Until those systems are firmly entrenched in the firm, you still just have a practice and not a business.

Now, you might be asking, "What's the point of all this systemization? Any attorney knows how to file a brief just as any receptionist knows how to greet clients."

And that might be true.

But that doesn't mean they know "your way." You might have some different ideas about how to best get things done, and if you're really interested in transforming your practice into a self-sufficient business, you most certainly should have some different ideas.

Your completion plan makes sure that everyone is on the same page. It ensures that your clients are always greeted in the same manner, even if your receptionist is not available to do the greeting. It guarantees that any brief produced by your law firm gets filed and documented in an efficient and timely manner.

Your completion plan allows your practice to evolve by constantly questioning the "way we've always done things" and then looking for the "way we should be doing things" instead.

And when you implement this type of game plan, everyone in your firm can get on board. Suddenly, instead of having "people issues," you have system issues, but now you and your staff can tackle those issues together and that creates a major shift in the way you do business.

Your staff will feel more confident about the way they do their job and your vendors and clients will reap the benefits of your efficiency.

Your plan will identify the goal you want to accomplish, outline the steps required to do it, and establish a system for tracking those steps and monitoring performance. In the world of management, there is no easier way to stay on top of your business than this.

And when you implement these systems, you'll find that it's much easier to position your firm as a leader in the marketplace. Trust us on this—we've seen it happen over and over again.

At the American Academy of Estate Planning Attorneys, we utilize a practice management program known as the "11 Essential Systems to Dominate Your Market." It looks something like this:

- **Strategic Planning System**—Aligning your business with your personal values
- **Integrated Client Marketing System**—Multiple marketing activities generating an endless supply of qualified prospects
- **No-Stress Client Engagement System**—Predictably inspiring clients to take action and retain your firm
- **Dependable Client Services System**—Drafting, presenting, and executing state-of-the-art estate plans
- **Lifetime Communication System**—Regularly communicating with clients through multiple touches

- **Continuity Revenue System**—Dependable income year after year from every client
- **Comprehensive Technology System**—Integration of the best tools to draft documents and manage your firm
- **Staff Accountability and Team-Building System**—Putting the right people with the right skills in the right positions
- **Financial Management System**—Managing by the numbers to keep in touch with your profitability
- **Continuing Legal Education System**—Staying on the cutting edge of effective legal strategies
- **Ancillary Business System**—Developing multiple sources of revenue

This "system of systems" provides our members with the tools they need to address every aspect of practice management without getting lost in a long list of to-do's. And as we watch the firms we coach implement these systems, we see the transformation from practice to business begin.

With the planning process out of the way, you can start putting your ideas into action, and that means management. So, let's keep going in our transformational journey and learn how to manage all these plans you've created.

www.michaelegerber.com/attorney

CHAPTER

7

On the Subject of
Management

Michael E. Gerber

*"Management" means, in the last analysis, the substitution of thought
for brawn and muscle, of knowledge for folklore and superstition, and of
cooperation for force.*

—Peter Drucker, *People and Performance*

E very attorney, including Edward, eventually faces the issues
of management. Yet most face it badly.

Why do so many attorneys suffer from a kind of
paralysis when it comes to dealing with management? Why are
so few able to get their legal practice to work the way they want it to
and to run it on time? Why are their managers (if they have any)
seemingly so inept?

The main problem is that more often than not, the attorney
doesn't think like a manager because he doesn't think he *is* a
manager. He's an attorney! He rules the roost. He may even hire
an office manager to take care of stuff like scheduling appointments,

57

keeping his calendar, collecting receivables, hiring/firing, and much more. But he is the king, and he subscribes to the Latin maxim he learned in law school: *Rex non fit malum*, the king can do no wrong.

No matter who does the managing, attorneys usually have a completely dysfunctional idea of what it means to manage. They're trying to manage people in a way that is contrary to what is needed (to the extent that they're even focused on the concept at all).

We often hear that a good manager must be a "people person." Someone who loves to nourish, figure out, support, care for, teach, baby, monitor, mentor, direct, track, motivate, and, if all else fails, threaten or beat up her people.

Don't believe it. Management has far less to do with people than you've been led to believe.

In fact, despite the claims of every management book written by management gurus (who have seldom managed anything), no one—with the exception of a few bloodthirsty tyrants—has ever learned how to manage people.

And the reason is simple: *People are almost impossible to manage*.

Yes, it's true. People are unmanageable. They're inconsistent, unpredictable, unchangeable, unrepentant, irrepressible, and generally impossible.

Doesn't knowing this make you feel better? Now you understand why you've had all those problems! Do you feel the relief, the heavy stone lifted from your chest?

The time has come to fully understand what management is really all about. Rather than managing *people*, management is really all about managing a *process*, a step-by-step way of doing things, which, combined with other processes, becomes a system. For example:

- The process for on-time scheduling
- The process for answering the telephone
- The process for greeting a client
- The process for organizing client files

Thus, a process is the step-by-step way of doing something over time. Considered as a whole, these processes are a system:

The on-time scheduling system

The telephone answering system

The client greeting system

The file organization system

Instead of managing people, then, the truly effective manager has been taught a system for managing a process through which people get things done.

More precisely, managers and their people, *together*, manage the processes—the systems—that comprise your business. Management is less about *who* gets things done in your business than about *how* things get done.

In fact, great managers are not fascinated with people, but with how things get done through people. Great managers are masters at figuring out how to get things done effectively and efficiently through people using extraordinary systems.

You don't need to be Vince Lombardi, his heart on his sleeve as he coached the Green Bay Packers.

Instead, you need to be Tom Landry, displaying the cool and resolve of his background as a bomber pilot during World War II and his engineering degree.

You don't need to wear the fedora on the sidelines. You do need to be clear about your systems, so that your team can do it your way consistently . . . and win.

Great managers constantly ask key questions:

- What is the result we intend to produce?
- Are we producing that result every single time?
- If we're not producing that result every single time, why not?
- If we are producing that result every single time, how could we produce even better results?

- Do we lack a system? If so, what would that system look like if we were to create it?
- If we have a system, why aren't we using it?

And so forth.

In short, a great manager can leave the office fully assured that it will run at least as well as it does when he or she is physically in the room.

Great managers are those who use a great management system. Such a system shouts, "This is *how* we manage here!" not, "This is *who* manages here!"

In a truly effective company, how you manage is always more important than who manages. Provided that a system is in place, how you manage is transferable, whereas who manages isn't. *How* you manage can be taught, whereas *who* manages can't be.

When a company is dependent on *who* manages—Murray, Mary, or Moe—that business is in serious jeopardy. Because when Murray, Mary, or Moe leaves, that business has to start over again. What an enormous waste of time and resources!

Even worse, when a company is dependent on *who* manages, you can bet all the managers in that business are doing their own thing. What could be more unproductive than ten managers who each manage in a unique way? How in the world could you possible manage those managers?

The answer is clear: You can't, because it takes you right back to trying to manage *people* again.

And, as I hope you now know, that's impossible.

In this chapter, I often refer to managers in the plural. I know that most attorneys only have one manager, the office manager, if they have any at all. And so you may be thinking that a management system isn't so important in a small legal practice. After all, the office manager does whatever an office manager does (and thank God because you don't want to do it).

But if your practice is ever going to turn into the business it could become, and if that business is ever going to turn into the enterprise of your dreams, then the questions you ask about how the office manager manages your affairs are critical ones. Until you come to grips with your dual role as owner and key employee, and the relationship that your manager has to those two roles, your practice/business/enterprise will never realize its potential. Thus, the need for a management system.

Management System

What, then, is a management system?

The E-Myth says that a management system is the method by which every manager innovates, quantifies, orchestrates, and then monitors the systems through which your practice produces the results you expect.

According to the E-Myth, a manager's job is simple:

A manager's job is to invent the systems through which the owner's vision is consistently and faithfully manifested at the operating level of the business.

Which brings us right back to the purpose of your business and the need for an entrepreneurial vision.

Are you beginning to see what I'm trying to share with you? That your business is one single thing? And that all the subjects we're discussing here—money, planning, management, and so on—are all about doing one thing well?

That one thing is the one thing your practice is intended to do: distinguish your legal business from all others.

It is the manager's role to make certain it all fits. And it's your role as entrepreneur to make sure that your manager knows what the business is supposed to look, act, and feel like when it's finally done. As clearly as you know how, you must convey to your manager what you know to be true—your vision, your picture of the business when it's finally done. In this way, your vision is translated into your manager's marching orders every day he or she reports to work.

Unless that vision is embraced by your manager, you and your people will suffer from the tyranny of routine. And your business will suffer from it, too.

Now let's move on to *people*. Because, as we know, it's people who are causing all our problems. But first, let's listen to what Robert and Sandy have to say about management.

www.michaelegerber.com/attorney

CHAPTER 8

Managing the Unmanageable

Robert Armstrong
Sanford M. Fisch

So much of what we call management consists in making it difficult for people to work.

—Peter Drucker

Anyone in the business of "doing business" has read at least one book on the topic. And chances are, that book dealt specifically with the subject of management, most likely because there are so many to choose from.

Take a quick trip to your local bookstore and you'll find an overwhelming selection of texts, all promising to reveal the most current trends in management strategies. Dig a little deeper and you'll discover that "management strategy" usually translates into motivating your employees.

Because that's really what "management" is all about isn't it— overseeing the people who work for you? The problem is, you end up having to play the role of part-time psychiatrist, babysitter, priest, and warden to make these complex systems work.

But what if we've been focused on the wrong problem? What if your people weren't the issue? What if it was your systems instead? That puts a whole new spin on things, doesn't it?

Because now, instead of trying to manage a group of distinctly unique individuals—all of whom by the way, have their own set of ideas, motivators and emotions—you can now manage a set of systems, which are analytical, not emotional. Systems don't require motivation or nurturing to work, and are designed by you.

This breakthrough way of thinking was first presented by Michael Gerber in his book, *E-Myth*. He discovered it while observing the extraordinary success of fast food pioneer, McDonald's. Somehow, they needed to turn pimply-faced, ADD, teenaged kids into productive workers in charge of multimillion-dollar franchises and you know what? They did it!

As Michael describes it, "They come in late, leave early and smoke dope during lunch." They have a thousand-percent turnover of employees, and still these same workers produce record profits and make a McDonald's franchise the closest thing to owning a money-making machine.

So, how did they accomplish such an impossible feat? Certainly not by trying to control hormone-ravaged teenagers, but rather by focusing on the systems for doing things with a step-by-step written blueprint for every task. The steps for making french fries, greeting customers, cleaning up, and tracking cash are documented in detail for every staff member to see. In short, a written manual that most likely includes multimedia learning tools provides documentation and training for every new hire who walks through the door. If one worker leaves, a new one can be up and running, producing identical results whether they're in Buffalo or Bangkok. Now that's a system!

You might be wondering what this has to do with you and your not-so-juvenile staff. In a word, everything. In fact, it doesn't matter whether you're a doctor, a contractor, a banker, or a retail firm, any business will benefit when they choose to manage systems rather than people.

That's not to say that the high-quality personnel in your firm isn't valuable—they most certainly are. But the majority of your focus should still be on creating innovative systems that you can measure and monitor. Once those systems are in place, it becomes much easier to find world-class employees who can make them work. And what's more, employees who might otherwise have been passed over often blossom into productive staff members when given a turnkey system like the one we're describing here. We've seen it happen over and over again. This makes hiring new employees a much easier prospect.

Attorneys are often obsessed with finding experienced workers, from receptionists, paralegals, and file clerks, to bookkeepers and yes, even other attorneys in the firm. We take a different view. Find people with the right personalities and character traits for each type of job—people who possess key attributes that can't be taught, like friendliness, perseverance, and great interpersonal skills, balanced with an eagerness to learn and a desire to take on responsibility— and then marry those people to your set of innovative systems and watch your firm begin to transform!

Obviously, you'll want to have workers who possess basic skills in their field, but in all honesty, most of those skills can be taught. We find that it's easier to teach a bright, inexperienced paralegal the skills they'll need in your law firm than to try to undo the bad habits that a more experienced person might bring from some other dysfunctional firm. Those are the employees who resist change, which means they're also resisting growth. Tell them thanks, but no thanks, and move on. Your firm and your innovative staff will thank you for it.

When we audit a law firm, we routinely ask the attorneys to describe the positions in their firm and the employees who currently hold the jobs. The conversation invariably goes the same way. They'll describe the personalities, work habits, and general opinions about each employee.

But we've never once heard an attorney talk about the systems in place that represent how they do things in their firm. They might lament Mary's shortcomings or sing Tom's praises, but that's where the analysis stops. And interestingly, they don't realize that even if they had a firm filled with Toms, they would be no closer to having a well-managed business.

The reason they don't realize this is because Tom is doing his job and it's a great job at that. But someday, Tom will leave the firm, just like every other great employee you might have working for you at this very moment. Whether it's because of illness, a move, a better job, pregnancy, or some other reason, it's rare that an employee spends her or his entire career with the same entity.

When the great employee does decide to leave, the attorney suddenly realizes that all that wisdom and experience they held so dear has just walked out the door. What to do, what to do?

Tom knew where all the files were kept. He knew how to set up the conference room or pay the vendors or draft a brief and get it filed with the court before day's end. But now Tom's gone. And since even the best employees typically give a whole two weeks notice, you don't have much time to replace your star employee.

So, tell us—can you possibly recruit, hire, and train that replacement in two weeks? Probably not. Which means that your best worker just crippled your law firm. Not intentionally of course, but that's still the way it worked out. Had your systems been in place, however, training a replacement would be a snap. Tom's leaving wouldn't equate to years of knowledge lost. Your firm would not only survive Tom leaving, but it would continue to prosper as well.

We see it happen all the time. And we'll tell you just like we tell the law firms we've worked with: Without systems, your best workers are potentially your biggest obstacle to having a great business.

Crafting a New Vision

With the right systems, your law firm will be re-created to reflect your vision about practicing law. What is going to make your firm unique?

Why should prospective clients pick your firm over all others? What special place will your practice occupy in the community?

In the beginning, maybe it was just about the money. Get the clients in the door and start generating as many fees as you can. But we all know that's not a sustainable business model and, more importantly, will not ultimately serve you or your clients.

But when you implement systems, you create the machine that can work independently of you. You give your employees the roadmap they need to do the things that need to get done.

- This is how we greet clients.
- This is how we draft documents.
- This is how we take a deposition.
- This is how we prepare for trial.
- This is how we manage our finances.
- This is how we generate leads and convert them into retained clients.
- This is how we hire great people.

And so on and so on . . .

What's this got to do with your staff and your team? Everything. Because unless you can give your people a predictable detailed system in which to operate, they'll wing it on their own. Human nature will take over and one person will do the job one way while another does it her way, until you end up with a chaotic free-for-all and the original vision you had for a predictable, consistent expression of your way of practicing law will vanish.

If you go back and look at the planning process we discussed earlier, you'll quickly see that the "what" is far more important than the "who." But before you can have a business that truly serves your needs, you need to know what that business is. You need to define the "what" piece of your firm's puzzle. Now that we've established the importance of managing your systems, let's see how that plays with the people in your firm.

www.michaelegerber.com/attorney

On the Subject of People

Michael E. Gerber

We are not human beings having a spiritual experience.
We are spiritual beings having a human experience.
—Teilhard de Chardin

Every attorney I've ever met has complained about people.
About employees: "They come in late, they go home
early, they have the focus of an antique camera!"

About partners and associates: "Who knows what they do with
their time—but they certainly know how to bill it! And getting
them to turn in their billable hours is like pulling teeth!"

About paralegals: "They're living in a nonparallel universe!"

About clients: "They want me to rewrite the law to suit their
individual whims!"

People, people, people. Every attorney's nemesis. And at the
heart of it all are the people who work for you.

"By the time I tell them how to do it, I could have done it
twenty times myself!" "How come nobody listens to what I say?"
"Why is it nobody ever does what I ask them to do?" Does this
sound like you?

So what's the problem with people? To answer that, think back to the last time you walked into an attorney's office. What did you see in the people's faces?

Most people working in the legal profession, I'm sure you will agree, are harried. You can see it in their expressions. They're negative. They're bad-spirited. They're humorless. And with good reason. After all, the clients who trudge in and out of the office each day have a lot to deal with. Whether they're filing a lawsuit, signing divorce papers, or drawing up a final will and testament, people typically don't head down to the local law office for a good time. Most clients are worried, angry, or anxious; they may even be terrified or depressed. Thus, the employees of every legal practice are constantly surrounded by unhappy people.

Is it any wonder these employees are disgruntled? They're answering the same questions all day from people who don't want to be there. And most of the time, the attorney has no time for them. He or she is too busy leading a dysfunctional life.

Working with people brings great joy—and monumental frustration. And so it is with attorneys and their people. But why? And what can we do about it?

Let's look at the typical attorney—who this person is and isn't. Most attorneys are unprepared to use other people to get results. Not because they can't find people, but because they are fixated on getting the results themselves. In other words, most attorneys are not the businesspeople they need to be, but *technicians suffering from an entrepreneurial seizure.*

Am I talking about you? What were you doing before you became an entrepreneur? Were you an associate lawyer working at a large firm? A mid-sized firm? A boutique firm? Were you in-house somewhere?

Didn't you imagine owning your own practice as the way out? Didn't you think that because you knew how to do the technical work—because you knew so much about probate or entertainment law or immigration—that you were automatically prepared to create a practice that does that type of work?

Didn't you figure that by creating your own practice you could dump the boss once and for all? How else to get rid of that impossible person, the one driving you crazy, the one who never let you do your own thing, the one who was the main reason you decided to take the leap into a business of your own in the first place?

Didn't you start your own practice so that you could become your own boss? And didn't you imagine that once you became your own boss, you would be free to do whatever you wanted to do—and to take home *all* the money?

Honestly, isn't that what you imagined? So you went into business for yourself and immediately dove into work.

Doing it, doing it, doing it. Busy, busy, busy. Until one day you realized (or maybe not) that you were doing all of the work. You were doing everything you knew how to do, plus a lot more you knew nothing about. Building sweat equity, you thought. In reality, a technician suffering from an entrepreneurial seizure.

You were just hoping to make a decent living in your own practice. Actually, you hoped for considerably more than that. You wanted to beat the big firms at their own game. And sometimes you did earn a nice dollar. But other times you didn't. You were the one signing the checks all right, but they went to other people.

Does this sound familiar? Is it driving you crazy? Well, relax, because we're going to show you the right way to do it this time.

Read carefully. Be mindful of the moment. You are about to learn the secret you've been waiting for all your working life.

The People Law

It's critical to know this about the working life of attorneys who own their own legal practice: *Without people, you don't own a practice, you own a job.* And it can be the worst job in the world because you're working for a lunatic! (Nothing personal—we simply have to face the truth if we're ever going to change things.)

Let me state what every attorney knows: Without people, you're going to have to do it all yourself. Without human help, you're doomed to try to do too much. This isn't a breakthrough idea, but it's amazing how many attorneys ignore the truth. They end up knocking themselves out, twelve to sixteen hours a day. They try to do more, but less actually gets done.

The load can double you over and leave you panting. In addition to the work you're used to doing, you may also have to do the books. And the organizing. And the filing. You'll have to do the planning and the scheduling. In a legal practice of your own, the daily minutiae is never-ceasing—as I'm sure you've found out—and until you discover how to get it done by somebody else, it will continue on and on until you're a burned-out husk.

Like painting the Golden Gate Bridge, it's endless. Which puts it beyond the realm of human possibility.

But with others helping you, my attorney friend, things will start to drastically improve. If, that is, you truly understand how to engage people in the work you need them to do. When you learn how to do that, when you learn how to replace yourself with other people—people trained in your system—then your practice can really begin to grow. Only then will you begin to experience true freedom yourself.

What typically happens is that attorneys, knowing they need help answering the phone, filing, and so on, go out and find people who can do these things. Once they delegate these duties, however, they rarely spend any time with the hoi polloi. Deep down they feel it's not important *how* these things get done; it's only important that they get done.

They fail to grasp the requirement for a system that makes people their greatest asset rather than their greatest liability. A system so reliable that if Mary dropped dead tomorrow, Judy could do exactly what Mary did. That's where the *people law* comes in.

The people law says that each time you add a new person to your practice using an intelligent (turnkey) system that works, you expand your reach. And you can expand your reach almost infinitely! People allow you to be everywhere you want to be simultaneously, without actually having to be there in the flesh.

People are to an attorney what a record was to Frank Sinatra. As we discussed earlier, a Sinatra record could be (and still is) played in a million places at the same time, regardless of where Frank was. And every record sale produced royalties for Sinatra (or his estate).

With the help of other people, Sinatra created a quality recording that faithfully replicated his unique talents, and then made sure it was marketed, distributed, and the revenue managed.

While Sinatra sang do-be-do-be-do, all *you* get to do . . . is do. And the result, alas, is doo-doo.

Your people can do the same thing for you. All *you* need to do is to create a "recording"—a system—of your unique talents, your special way of practicing law, and then replicate it, market it, distribute it, and manage the revenue.

Isn't that what successful businesspeople do? Make a "recording" of their most effective ways of doing business? In this way, they provide a turnkey solution to their clients' problems. A system solution that really works.

Doesn't your practice offer the same potential for you that records did for Frank Sinatra (and now for his heirs)? The ability to produce income without having to go to work every day? Isn't that what your people could be for you? The means by which your system for practicing law could be faithfully replicated?

But first you've got to have a system. You have to create a unique way of doing business that you can teach to your people, that you can manage faithfully, and that you can replicate consistently, just like McDonald's.

Without such a system, without such a "recording," without a unique way of doing business that really works, all you're left with is people doing their own thing. And that is almost always a recipe for chaos. Rather than guaranteeing consistency, it encourages mistake after mistake after mistake.

And isn't that how the problem started in the first place? People doing whatever *they* perceived they needed to do, regardless of what you wanted? People left to their own devices, with no regard for the costs of their behavior? The costs to you? In other words, people without a system.

Can you imagine what would have happened to Frank Sinatra if he had followed that example? If every one of his recordings had been done differently? Imagine a million different versions of "My Way." It's unthinkable.

Would you buy a record like that? What if Frank was having a bad day? What if he had a sore throat?

Please hear this: The people law is unforgiving. Without a systematic way of doing business, people are more often a liability than an asset. Unless you prepare, you'll find out too late which ones are which.

The people law says that without a specific system for doing business; without a specific system for recruiting, hiring, and training your people to use that system; and without a specific system for managing and improving your systems, your practice will always be a crapshoot.

Do you want to roll the dice with your practice at stake? Unfortunately, that is what most attorneys are doing.

The people law also says that you can't effectively delegate your responsibilities unless you have something specific to delegate. And that something specific is a way of doing business that works!

Frank Sinatra is gone, but his voice lives on. And someone is still counting his royalties. That's because Sinatra had a system that worked.

Do you? Do you get to be as well as to do? Do, be, do, be, do? Or are you just doing, all day long?

Now let's move on to the subject of *associate lawyers*. But first, let's listen to what Robert and Sandy have to say about people.

www.michaelegerber.com/attorney

CHAPTER 10

People Needing People

Robert Armstrong
Sanford M. Fisch

Good management consists in showing average people how to do the work of superior people.

—John D. Rockefeller

With your systems firmly in place, you can now turn your attention to the backbone of your business, also known as your people.

For years we've been telling attorneys that properly trained staff, including paralegals, can accomplish a big percentage of what must be done in a law firm, and we still stand by this notion. Too many lawyers are doing things that are better left to staff, and the result is that the firm doesn't run as smoothly as it could, regardless of how well you think you're managing the workload.

But as Michael so eloquently put it, "Without people, you don't own a practice—you own a job."

Certainly, for some lawyers, having a high-paying job is exactly what they want and they do this by working in someone else's firm where they can focus on the doing it, doing it, doing it, while other "people" handle everything else. They spend their days taking depositions, arguing cases, attending CLE conferences, and honing their legal skills. And there's nothing wrong with that.

But if you aspire to owning your own shop—or perhaps want to revamp the one you have—you gave up that employee mentality a long time ago. You wanted to control your own destiny, come and go as you please, say yes to some clients and show others the door. You wanted the entrepreneurial life with all its potential payoffs and riches.

But going from employee to business owner wasn't as easy as it seemed. You work longer than ever before, often with very little to show for your efforts, and your stress level has increased exponentially from that of your days as an employee, not to mention the havoc it's created in your personal life.

Fortunately, this is where people can help. Not just any people, of course, but *your people.*

The Faces of Your Firm

Essentially, there are three categories of workers in your firm: managers, lawyers, and support staff. Often the manager and the lawyer are one and the same, meaning that all the lawyer-related tasks get done while the managing aspect of the firm gets pushed to the backburner.

Granted, we all know there are some responsibilities in the firm that can only be performed by a licensed attorney. These are tasks that can't be delegated or outsourced, but we also know that too many attorneys are holding on to jobs that are better suited to trained staff. In the estate planning area, for example, we tell lawyers that they can free up almost half of their time just by delegating one job.

You can imagine how curious they are to learn what this job is! What could possibly free up that much time? Want to know what it is? Stop insisting on leading and attending the entire final meeting with clients to sign routine estate planning documents, such as wills and trusts. That job should be assigned to a well-trained paralegal with a winning personality.

Sounds simple in theory, but you would think we had just asked them to surrender their law license. Of course, they have a dozen reasons for why it wouldn't work, all of which we've heard a hundred times before.

So we wait. We let them tell us how ridiculous the idea is, and then when they're through, we ask them to try it for one month. Just one month and see what happens. And after all these years, we've never had a single attorney declare that the old way was better . . . not one!

What makes this change work is having a system in place to handle this task. There is no legal reason that an attorney must be present while the client signs those documents—they've just assumed that their presence was needed because only they knew what needed to be done.

But once the system is established, any good paralegal can handle the process without blinking an eye. And for the technician in you who's screaming, "That won't work," yes, there are some exceptions to the rule. But you're missing the point—delegating tasks that don't require your personal attention can free up your calendar.

And that means more time for the attorney to work on all those attorney-only issues. Just by making that one change, these attorneys have expanded their ability to do business efficiently. And should that paralegal one day decide to leave, you now have a system in place that allows your new paralegal to pick up right where the other one left off.

This is the real secret behind business success. Because not only does your business run more efficiently, but your staff becomes happier as well. And who doesn't want a happy staff? Remember, your paralegal chose that career path because he or she wanted to do paralegal kinds of things, not just sit around and answer a phone—just like you became an attorney because you wanted to practice law, not fill your days with clerical duties.

Yes, you're perfectly capable of doing many of those paralegal tasks yourself, but most attorneys will agree that a properly trained paralegal who loves being with people is better at that job than they are. Plus, now your clients get to bond with your firm—not just you—so when they have routine questions, they'll be comfortable talking to your paralegal instead of insisting on speaking to you personally. Can you see just how much time you could save by making this one little change?

Our perspective is that if a task does not legally require a lawyer—meaning it's not considered to fall under the practice of law, then a non-lawyer is often the best choice for the job. And we'll tell you another secret: This rule always holds true.

Once you've implemented your systems, you can address the issue of who will do what. And this is where "management" can really be fun. Filling the positions in your firm is similar to working a jigsaw puzzle. You want the right piece in the right place for the puzzle to come together as a whole.

In his best seller, *Good to Great*, author Jim Collins illustrates this concept by comparing your firm to people on a bus. He said you must not only have the right people on your bus, but they must also be in the right seats. An all-too-common example is having a painfully shy person sitting at the front desk with the responsibility of greeting clients and answering the phones when the person you really want in that position is a friendly, warm, outgoing individual who loves people. Someone who puts people at ease, makes them feel comfortable and has the ability to naturally establish trust.

Ironically, the front desk position is often an afterthought for attorneys, when in truth, it's that position that essentially holds the key to your firm's first impression. Many lawyers make a big mistake by putting the least-qualified people in that spot and then paying them poorly to boot. But remember, the front desk is often the first contact that prospects and clients have with your firm, so you definitely want someone who is suited to welcome people into your office.

And this is true with any position in your firm. As you start fitting people with your various systems, make sure you look beyond skills and match personalities and talents to the job as well.

When you do this, you create a staff that has a vested interest in your firm's success. They know that their job is an integral part of your law practice, even if they aren't actually practicing law.

This knowledge instills things like pride and loyalty—qualities that most certainly can transform an office full of "people" into an efficient and innovative staff. Now, which one would you like to work with?

This process of bringing people on board is essentially your hiring system. It will outline how you solicit candidates, how they are interviewed, and what tests should be administered, as well as how you'll check references and do background investigations.

One incredibly valuable part of a good hiring system is something called a "group interview." For most positions in the firm this method will save lots of time for both you and the candidates. We have taught this system for years and, like delegating the final signing meeting, it was resisted at first until the attorneys saw how it quickly zeroed in on the people you really wanted to interview one-on-one.

And here's why it works: When you have a position to be filled in your firm, a series of events must take place. An ad appears, whether it's in the newspaper or on the web, and interested candidates send in their resumes. You review the qualifications and schedule individual interviews. This can be incredibly time consuming, and if your experiences are like ours, some people don't show up, and in the case of others, you wish they hadn't bothered.

But of course, we rarely terminate the interview within the first few minutes, even when we know it's a waste of time because we feel obligated to "hear them out."

But in a group interview, you invite all of the candidates who pass the first round of resume reviews in at the same time. You set up a room at your firm (your delightful receptionist could handle that task for you!) and you or a trusted staff member makes a presentation about your firm, its culture, and the nature of the position you're offering. Once the introduction is done, you can now ask the group if there is anyone who is not interested in the job. For those who remain, and in our experience it will be most of them, you can start asking open-ended questions to the applicants.

And here's where the magic begins. Something remarkable happens in the "back and forth" that goes on between the people in the room. You get an opportunity to see how they interact with each other and with your team. You get to see whether they are outgoing, articulate, reserved, how they dress, how they carry themselves, and a hundred other little characteristics that you might not have seen in a one-on-one. Once the meeting is over, you can huddle with your team and decide which of the group are worthy of a further interview. All those who would never have made the cut are skimmed off early. Again, this is one of those best practices that attorneys initially resist but totally embrace once they give it a try. It's also another example of why it's important to rethink the way you do business.

Now, all this glowing hype aside, you must still have a system for personality and skill testing of the candidates, even with the group interview method. This is because most people hire for all the wrong reasons. Some like the candidate and go with their gut, while others tend to hire employees who are just like them. Most often people are under a time crunch and simply don't bother with the investigation part of the process.

Typically, this happens because there is no system in place for hiring. What's more, often there are no systems in place at all. As a result, there is a huge panic when someone leaves. The firm feels the need to fill the position quickly, which usually amounts to getting a warm body in that chair.

But as we've already seen, this is a recipe for disaster, a recipe you won't be following anymore, will you? Now, just because you've found the person you want to hire doesn't mean the hiring process is over. Quite the contrary, there's still much to do with a new employee—see why a few good systems can come in handy?

A new employee needs to be introduced to your firm's benefit package if you have one. Someone needs to ensure that he fills out all the appropriate forms and that accounting is notified of his employment so that he can get paid.

You then need another system to ensure that what you hired is truly what you wanted. And this is where monitoring those systems can help you out.

No matter how much you test or how much you interview, you can never be certain you've made the right decision until they're actually on the job! After over fifty years of combined experience in hiring employees, we know that the best you can do is increase the odds of a proper hire by going through all the steps we've just outlined above. But even then, there are no guarantees.

To counter this uncertainty, you're going to use some of those glorious systems to help you monitor your new employee's progress and ensure that they're truly a good fit for your firm. To do this, you'll need to create a set of questions that the new hire answers each day for the first twenty days of employment. You can decide what the questions are for your firm, but here are a few that have worked for us:

- Did you understand what was expected of you today?
- Were you able to accomplish your work today?
- What challenges did you face?
- What resources do you need to help you do your job better?

During those first twenty days, have the new employee send you a report answering those questions. In addition to providing the answers you need, this daily procedure will also show you whether the person can follow instructions and whether she is comfortable with reporting her activities.

A major problem we've seen in law firms is that the lawyers and/or management do not take the time to follow up with their new hires. These new employees are simply shown to their desk and given their list of responsibilities—the rest is up to them.

But this is the time when coaching and feedback are the most effective. Your new employee hasn't developed any systems of his own yet, so now is the time to stay close and guide him along.

This is also the time that you can determine if you made the right choice. Granted, all new people will have a learning curve, but if you're not seeing the performance you expected, well, what you see is generally what you get.

Which then leaves you with two choices: Keep the mediocre employee around to avoid having to hire someone new or cut that person loose and move on. Obviously, it's your call, but if you want the right people on your bus, you have to be willing to let a few get off.

Now that we've addressed the general aspect of hiring employees, let's get a little more specific and look at hiring other attorneys.

www.michaelegerber.com/attorney

On the Subject of Associates

Michael E. Gerber

All animals are equal, but some animals are more equal than others.
—George Orwell, *Animal Farm*

I f you're a sole practitioner—that is, you're selling only yourself—then your legal company called a practice will never make the leap to a legal company called a business. The progression from practice to business to enterprise demands that you hire other attorneys to do what you do (or don't do). Contractors call these people subcontractors; in the legal profession, they're known as associate lawyers.

Contractors know that subs can be a huge problem. It's no less true for attorneys. Until you face this special business problem, your practice will never become a business, and your business will certainly never become an enterprise.

Long ago, God said, "Let there be attorneys. And so they never forget who they are in my creation, let them be damned forever to hire people exactly like themselves." Enter the associates.

Merriam-Webster's Collegiate Dictionary, Eleventh Edition, defines "sub" as "under, below, secretly; inferior to." If associate lawyers are like sub-attorneys, you could define an associate as "an inferior individual contracted to perform part or all of another's contract."

In other words, you, the attorney, make a conscious decision to hire someone "inferior" to you to fulfill *your* commitment to *your* client, for which you are ultimately and solely liable.

Why in the world do we do these things to ourselves? Where will this madness lead? It seems the blind are leading the blind, and the blind are paying others to do it. Talk about an approach doomed to fail at the very outset!

It's time to step out of the darkness. It's time to see the world as it really is. It's time to do things that work.

Solving the Associate Lawyer Problem

Let's say you're about to hire an associate lawyer. Someone who has specific skills: bankruptcy law, malpractice, whatever. It all starts with choosing the right personnel. After all, these are people to whom you are delegating your responsibility and for whose behavior you are completely liable. Do you really want to leave that choice to chance? Are you that much of a gambler? I doubt it.

If you've never worked with your new associate, how do you really know he or she is skilled? For that matter, what does "skilled" mean? Good grades in law school? A footnote published in a Law Review? Or something more?

For you to make an intelligent decision about this associate lawyer, you must have a working definition of the word *skilled*. Your challenge is to know *exactly* what your expectations are, then to make sure your other attorneys operate with precisely the same expectations. Failure here almost ensures a breakdown in your relationship.

I want you to write the following on a piece of paper: "By *skilled*, I mean." Once you create your personal definition, it will become a standard for you and your practice, for your clients, and for your associate lawyers.

A standard, according to *Webster's Eleventh*, is something "set up and established by authority as a rule for the measure of quantity, weight, extent, value, or quality." Thus, your goal is to establish a measure of quality control, a standard of skill, which you will apply to all your associate lawyers. More important, you are also setting a standard for the performance of your company.

By creating standards for your selection of other attorneys—standards of skill, performance, integrity, financial stability, and experience—you have begun the powerful process of building a practice that can operate exactly as you expect it to. By carefully thinking about exactly what to expect, you have already begun to improve your practice.

In this enlightened state, you will see the selection of your associates as an opportunity to define what you (1) intend to provide for your clients, (2) expect from your employees, and (3) demand for your life.

Powerful stuff, isn't it? Are you up to it? Are you ready to feel your rising power?

Don't rest on your laurels just yet. Defining those standards is only the first step you need to take. The second step is to create an *associate lawyer development system.*

An associate lawyer development system is an action plan designed to tell you what you are looking for in an associate. It includes the exact benchmarks, accountabilities, timing of fulfillment, and budget that you will assign to the process of looking for associate lawyers, identifying them, recruiting them, interviewing them, training them, managing their work, auditing their performance, compensating them, reviewing them regularly, and terminating or rewarding them for their performance.

All of these things must be documented—actually *written down*—if they're going to make any difference to you, your associate lawyers, your managers, or your bank account! And then you've got to persist with that system, come hell or high water. Just as Ray Kroc did. Just as Walt Disney did. Just as Sam Walton did.

This leads us to our next topic of discussion: the subject of *estimating.* But first, let's listen to what Robert and Sandy have to say on the subject of associate lawyers.

www.michaelegerber.com/attorney

CHAPTER 12

The Lawyer's View

Robert Armstrong
Sanford M. Fisch

The best executive is one who has sense enough to pick good men to do what he wants done, and self-restraint enough to keep from meddling with them while they do it.

—Theodore Roosevelt

Building a law practice, and building a business are not synonymous. In fact, the two are actually very different.

Building a law practice has historically meant hiring more attorneys so that you can increase your billable hours. You do that by accommodating more clients, which ultimately increases your revenue, and thus makes your law practice a success.

Doesn't it?

If you're goal is in fact, to increase your billable hours, then yes, hiring more attorneys would probably be the fastest way to achieve that goal and reach your definition of "success."

But what if your goal is something bigger than that? What if you want to enjoy more flexibility in your own schedule? Give something back to the community? Improve your existing client's customer satisfaction level?

What if your definition of success is more than just a ton of billable hours? What then?

Ahh, see now we're talking about building a business and from this perspective, hiring associate attorneys has a whole new meaning.

After all, you're going to be responsible for that associate, something that, as Michael pointed out in the last chapter can be a hit or miss experience if you aren't diligent about choosing the right personnel.

You're not just looking for someone who can increase your billable hours—what you're looking for is someone who will be an asset to your firm. And yes, there is a difference.

Just about any associate can bill for services rendered but it takes a special person to fill the particular spot you have in mind. Remember pieces of the puzzle? The right person in the right seat?

But how do you know who to hire? And how do you know if an associate is really what your firm needs?

These are questions we hear often and our answer is always the same: Your firm will need an associate when it's ready to support an associate. What on earth does that mean?

Well, there's actually a couple of different ways to define "support," so let's start with the easiest one: Clearly, your firm will need to have enough work to keep a new associate busy—that's a given. Your firm will also need to generate enough income to pay your new associate without causing the firm any financial strain— another relatively obvious requirement.

So now let's go a little deeper. Do you really need more lawyers in your firm or just a more efficient way of doing things?

Now, we're not suggesting that adding an attorney to your staff isn't a good idea. It might be just what your firm needs to continue on its evolutionary path. But before you can make that decision, you should feel confident that you are utilizing your non-attorney staff to their full potential.

We mentioned this in an earlier chapter but it's worth mentioning again here—it makes no sense to hire an associate if you've got qualified non-attorney staff that could do the job instead. Which raises the question of how you see an associate fitting into your firm's big picture. What will her role be? How will she complement what you already do?

Obviously, if you're hiring an associate to handle tasks that could be assumed by your paralegal, you're not choosing the most efficient path. You're also almost certainly guaranteeing that your associate (and quite likely your paralegal) will eventually get frustrated and leave for greener, and perhaps more satisfying, pastures.

But let's assume that you do, in fact, have enough lawyer-only work to warrant hiring an associate. Let's also assume that you run a lean, mean machine and every member of your staff enjoys a rewarding, challenging position in your firm. Does that mean it's time to hire an associate?

Perhaps. But let's add one more definition to the word "support," and this time, we're going to go with its most literal translation— Can your firm provide the support that a new associate needs to succeed?

Working within the concept of building a business rather than a practice, a new associate will need training. He'll need access to support staff such as secretaries or paralegals. He'll need a system for managing his calendar, prioritizing his mail, and ensuring that his case files are managed appropriately.

And just like any other new employee, a new associate will need feedback and guidance as she acclimates herself to your way of doing business.

Is your firm in a position to provide these things? If you don't yet have your basic systems in place (like the ones we've already discussed), then your new associate will be nothing more than another random employee doing his or her own thing. Kind of defeats the purpose of hiring the associate, don't you think?

In addition to this type of general support, you'll also want to have a separate system that defines the role of the associate and how he fits into your firm. In Chapter 11, Michael referred to this as the associate lawyer development system, and if you're even toying with the idea of hiring more attorneys, this is one system you don't want to be without.

Just like the job descriptions you've created for other positions in your office, an associate lawyer development system will outline the basic duties and responsibilities assigned to new associates when they walk through the door.

I mean, you weren't just going to let them grab a case file and run with it, were you? The development system provides not only the goals and measures that they will be held to, but also the tools they'll need to succeed.

It includes everything from their pay scale and experience requirements to the methods that they should use to document a file, contact a client, and yes, report those billable hours. It gives you the ability to monitor their growth and more importantly, gives them the means for measuring their own performance, which is a positively empowering way to do business.

And since you were shooting for something more profound than just another law practice anyway, "empowering" is certainly a great place to start.

www.michaelegerber.com/attorney

CHAPTER

13

On the Subject of Estimating

Michael E. Gerber

Clarity of mind means clarity of passion, too; this is why a great and clear mind loves ardently and sees distinctly what it loves.

—Blaise Pascal

O ne of the greatest weaknesses of attorneys is accurately estimating how long meetings will take and then scheduling their clients accordingly. *Webster's Collegiate Dictionary* defines estimate as "a rough or approximate calculation." Anyone who has visited an attorney's waiting room knows that those estimates can be rough indeed.

Do you want to hire an attorney who gives you a rough approximation? Can you imagine making major life decisions about money or property or jail time based solely on a rough approximation? The results wouldn't be pretty.

Well, that's what most attorneys do. It seems they've grown accustomed to using the word *estimate* without thinking about

91

what it really means. Is it any wonder that most attorneys lose money?

Enlightened attorneys, in contrast, banish the word "estimate" from their vocabulary. When it comes to estimating, just say "no"!

Let's say a client named Ms. Ancona has come into your office for a consultation regarding a business transaction. You spend an hour with Ms. Ancona, giving her a brief overview of the laws in your state and the different options available to her. You describe your professional background and your fee structure. Then, Ms. Ancona asks for an estimate.

You smile and say confidently, "We don't make estimates, Ms. Ancona. We make *promises*."

"You make *what?*" Ms. Ancona exclaims, mouth agape. It's almost like you just told her you'd do the job for free!

"Promises," you reply nonchalantly. Because you know the truth about what you do: Your superb system allows you to make promises because you can keep them.

You now have Ms. Ancona's rapt attention.

"Ms. Ancona," you say warmly, "we stopped giving estimates a long time ago. We realize that an estimate is a rough approximation of cost and time. We feel that if we can't be more exact than that, we don't deserve to be in business."

As her jaw drops, you continue.

"So, Ms. Ancona, we no longer provide estimates. Now we define exactly what it will take to build your case, how much it will cost, how long it will take, and then we give you our *written promise* that what we have agreed upon is *exactly* what we will deliver. On price, on time, and with precisely the quality you would expect from the very best attorney in the country."

"But how can you do that?" Ms. Ancona says, just now regaining all muscular function.

You smile. "That's what we do, Ms. Ancona. But I'll tell you this: We can do it because we did our homework."

Do you think Ms. Ancona would hire you on the spot? You bet she would!

"But you can never be exact," attorneys have told me for years. "Close, maybe. But never exact."

And in many instances, that is true. The very nature of the legal system often makes it difficult if not impossible to calculate an exact cost for your services. The area of litigation is a perfect example, since settling a case is one thing but if it goes to trial? Well, how can you be "exact" about that?

And the answer is, sometimes you can't. Sometimes, the honest answer really is that your fee is $500 an hour and this might last a week or it might last a year. All bets are off—there's just no real way to tell.

But you can't go to work every day believing that your practice, the work you do, and the commitments you make are all too complex and unpredictable to be even partially exact. With a mind-set like that, you're doomed to run a sloppy ship. A ship that will eventually sink and suck you down with it.

This is so easy to avoid. Because sloppiness—in both thought and action—is the root cause of your frustrations. The solution to those frustrations is clarity. Clarity gives you the ability to set a clear direction, which fuels the momentum you need to grow your business. Clarity, direction, momentum—they all come from insisting on exactness.

But how do you create exactness in a hopelessly inexact world? Well, you could refuse to do any work that can't be controlled exactly but with a few exceptions, that's obviously not a realistic choice.

Fortunately, you have another option: Rather than just toss that hourly rate at a client as you explain that there's simply no way to control how high their costs might go, I suggest that you change your approach by compartmentalizing your services and reconsidering just what that hourly rate includes.

Perhaps you can charge a flat fee for your initial pleading and court appearance, for example. Maybe you create a service package that includes the various meetings, phone calls, and consultations that often occur at the beginning of that type of case. Can your hourly fee include a few phone calls or regular progress reports?

How can you restructure what you do to make it more predict-able? Obviously, this is easier to do in some areas than in others, but if you start breaking down the functions of your practice, you'll see that it can be done. Standard services within estate planning, for example, can often be accurately priced without much error. A divorce attorney should be able to offer fairly exact pricing for a no-fault divorce, and even a criminal defense lawyer can accurately calculate the price for a straightforward plea bargain.

Yes, you'll have caveats in place that allow you to start charging that open-ended hourly fee if something doesn't go as planned, but offering your clients even a small amount of control can mean the difference between collecting your fee on time and fighting for every penny that you earn.

What you cannot do, what you must refuse to do, from this day forward, is to allow yourself to operate with an inexact mind-set. It will lead you to ruin. Which leads us inexorably back to the word I have been using through this book: "systems."

I'm not suggesting that a *systems solution* will guarantee that you always perform exactly as promised. But I am saying that a systems solution will faithfully alert you when you're going off track, and will do it before you have to pay the price for it.

In short, with a systems solution in place, you'll be able to accurately predict more and estimate less, both because you have organized your practice to anticipate mistakes and because you have put into place the system to do something about those mistakes before they blow up.

There's this, as well: To make a promise you intend to keep places a burden on you and your managers to dig deeply into how you intend to keep it. Such a burden will transform your intentions and increase your attention to detail.

With the promise will come dedication. With dedication will come integrity. With integrity will come consistency. With con-sistency will come results you can count on. And results you can count on mean that you get exactly what you hoped for at the outset of your practice: the true pride of ownership that every attorney should experience.

This brings us to the subject of *clients*. Who are they? Why do they come to you? How can you identify yours? And who *should* your clients be? But first, let's listen to what Robert and Sandy have to say about estimating.

www.michaelegerber.com/attorney

Billing and Certainty

Robert Armstrong
Sanford M. Fisch

Simplicity, clarity, singleness: these are the attributes that give our lives power and vividness and joy.

—Richard Halloway

I f you're looking to get under an attorney's skin, whisper these two little words: "alternative billing." In fact, for most attorneys, there is nothing more repulsive, more unnatural, more outrageous than charging a flat fee for services rendered. They'll stick to their hourly billing, thank you very much. It's just the way God intended it to be.

But like it or not, the age of flat-fee legal services is rapidly approaching. Recently *BusinessWeek* online announced that one of the most prestigious law firms in the nation is adopting an alternative billing model and suggesting that the practice of hourly billing should be abandoned:

"Corporations have long complained about hourly billing by the law firms they retain, a practice that seems to reward attorneys for spending as much time as possible on an assignment. The subject comes up from time to time at law firms, too, with some already taking incremental steps away from watching the clock. Yet, especially for litigation, hourly billing has persisted as the primary way big law firms charge for their services.

"Now, Evan Chesler, the presiding partner at white-shoe firm Cravath, Swaine & Moore, tells *Business Week* he's on a mission to 'make the billable hour irrelevant,' even for lawsuits. Chesler's proclamation is significant. Where New York–based Cravath goes, other elite firms often follow. And Cravath, Chesler says, is 'trying more and more to come to alternative fee arrangements.' Typically, this involves charging a flat fee. The move isn't recession-related, Chesler says, although he acknowledges that the idea 'resonates much more now,' as clients try to adhere to tighter budgets. Cravath may be a winner, too, he says. 'Ultimately it could be more profitable—if we are as good as we think we are.'"

Uncertainty about legal fees has always been a major source of irritation with clients, and for good reason. There's nothing very reassuring about sitting in an attorney's office with the clock ticking, and attorney fees accruing at the rate of $250 to $500 per hour. In fact, it's just this kind of uncertainty that often results in clients reaching out for help in the do-it-yourself arena where results can be disastrous, but fees are certain.

So, how do we weigh in on this debate? Truth be told, we've been recommending the flat-fee model to estate planning attorneys for years. Why? Because the flat-fee model is the only model that provides certainty not only to the client but the attorney as well. It's a win-win situation.

From the client's standpoint, the flat-fee model offers the advantage of determining the exact costs of legal representation. With the ticking clock eliminated, clients feel much more relaxed and attorney meetings become much more productive. But even more important, clients feel that the entire experience of obtaining legal counsel is finally balanced in their favor. Using the flat-rate fee model, attorneys will no longer have a financial incentive to draw out a case unnecessarily just to make more money, a practice many clients assume to be the normal way of doing business for a law firm.

From the attorney's perspective, a flat-rate fee model has some distinct advantages: It simplifies the billing process and provides the attorney with more time to manage the client's case, it eliminates the need to track hours, and it allows the attorney to be more competitive in the marketplace.

But the single most important advantage of the flat-rate model is that it makes the attorney's business more efficient. Contrary to the billable-hour model that promotes inefficiency, the flat-rate model is built around efficiency. And as we've already seen, efficiency in your operation can only occur if there are written systems in place at every level of your business, systems that allow paralegals and other non-attorney staff members to handle certain matters in a timely and cost-efficient manner.

Systems and delegation will allow you to determine an accurate cost of your services and will enable you to develop a flat rate that is both realistic and competitive. Yes, there may be instances where a case takes more or less time than anticipated, but these will be the exception, not the rule and you'll find that they average out in the long run.

Another way to take advantage of flat-fee billing is to create "packages," by bundling services together and charging an appropriate fee. Your packages can offer clients a tiered approach to your services, such as a basic package, gold package, and a platinum package, for example, each offering a different bundle of services at a different cost.

These packages can also serve as a great marketing tool. Just create and trademark a unique name for each level of service to distinguish your firm from your competitors.

The goal here is not to nickel-and-dime clients with charges for every little thing. It creates animosity, resentment, and diminishes referrals. When your clients feel they have to choose between their budget for legal expenses and a phone call to see how things are going, there is something seriously wrong with the business model.

Instead, build a certain number of phone calls into your packages. When the client exceeds that number, they can purchase

100 The E-Myth Attorney

another block of time. Better still, calculate your services so that unlimited phone calls are included as part of the flat fee. Sure, some people will abuse it, but the hassles you eliminate, the referrals you generate, and the goodwill you create will be well worth the annoyance.

Want to take the idea of service one step further? Give your clients a money-back guarantee. No, you can't guarantee the outcome of the case but you can guarantee the level of service you'll provide, such as providing regular updates or returning phone calls within a certain amount of time.

Granted, some areas of law may prohibit this particular practice, but use it where you can. And yes, some clients may abuse this service too, but imagine the buzz if word got out that you offered a guarantee!

After all, other businesses have been doing it for years, so why not law firms? While you might think that service guarantees look much like a gimmick, they remain a powerful tool for the entrepreneurial law firm. Guarantees give clients a sense of control in an otherwise uncontrollable matter, and they shift some of the risk to the law firm, making the relationship more advantageous and therefore, more appealing for the client.

Do service guarantees work? Just ask Ungaretti & Harris, one of Chicago's leading mid-sized firms. The 1989 recession hit the Chicago legal community hard, particularly damaging the stellar reputation of Ungaretti & Harris. Five years later, the firm sought to revitalize its tarnished image, and sought out a bold strategy to regain its quality reputation.

According to Ross Fishman of Fishman Marketing in Illinois, "To get the legal and business communities focused on the firm's service and innovation, we developed the nation's first *written service* guarantee, leading to a **50% increase in revenue in 12 months** during a flat 1995 market, as the firm grew from 60 to 90 lawyers, becoming one of the nation's ten fastest-growing firms.

"Client retention soared, attorney retention quadrupled, and led to quickly developing a well-deserved national reputation for quality, innovation and client service. The program received numerous awards including the ABA's Ethics in Advertising award for the nation's best ad campaign, as well as the Legal Marketing Association's grand prize in 1996, the optional Best of Show award, for the nation's best marketing campaign."

A major revolution is taking place throughout the world today. Businesses of all sizes are committed to return to a customer-centric environment. The legal profession needs to become part of that revolution.

Do everything possible to create a level of certainty in the minds of your clients. Bundle your services and offer flat fees. Provide your clients with a service guarantee. Make all your communications with the client understandable in plain English. Write with the client's interests in mind, not using legal jargon to make people think you're smart. Break concepts down so that clients understand what's happening with their case. It will eliminate unnecessary calls to the office and keep clients informed and happy.

Remember: Systems, predictability, consistency, and efficiency result in a legal business that is on the fast track to success.

www.michaelegerber.com/attorney

On the Subject of Clients

Michael E. Gerber

Lawyers' gowns are lined with the willfulness of their clients.

—Proverb

When it comes to the practice of law, the best definition of clients I've ever heard is this: *Clients—Very special people who drive most attorneys crazy.*

Does that work for you? After all, it's a rare client who shows any appreciation for what an attorney has to go through to do the job as promised. Don't they always think the price is too high? And don't they focus on problems, broken promises, and the mistakes they think you make, rather than all the times you bend over backward to give them what they need?

Do you ever hear other attorneys voice these complaints? More to the point, have you ever voiced them yourself? Well, you're not alone. I have yet to meet an attorney who doesn't suffer from a strong case of client confusion.

Client confusion is about:

- What your client really wants
- How to communicate effectively with your client
- How to keep your client happy
- How to deal with client dissatisfaction
- Whom to call a client

Confusion 1: What Does Your Client Really Want?

Your clients aren't just people; they're very specific kinds of people. Let me share with you the six categories of clients as seen from the E-Myth marketing perspective: (1) tactile clients, (2) neutral clients, (3) withdrawal clients, (4) experimental clients, (5) transitional clients, and (6) traditional clients.

Your entire marketing strategy must be based on which type of client you are dealing with. Each of the six client types spends money on legal services for very different, and identifiable, reasons. These are:

1. Tactile clients get their major gratification from interacting with other people.
2. Neutral clients get their major gratification from interacting with inanimate objects (a computer, a car, information).
3. Withdrawal clients get their major gratification from interacting with ideas (thoughts, concepts, stories).
4. Experimental clients rationalize their buying decisions by perceiving that what they bought is new, revolutionary, and innovative.
5. Transitional clients rationalize their buying decisions by perceiving that what they bought is dependable and reliable.
6. Traditional clients rationalize their buying decisions by perceiving that what they bought is cost-effective, a good deal, and worth the money.

In short:

1. If your client is tactile, you have to emphasize the *people* of your practice.

2. If your client is neutral, you have to emphasize the *technology* of your practice.

3. If your client is a withdrawal client, you have to emphasize the *idea* of your practice.

4. If your client is an experimental client, you have to emphasize the *uniqueness* of your practice.

5. If your client is transitional, you have to emphasize the *dependability* of your practice.

6. If your client is traditional, you have to talk about the *financial competitiveness* of your practice.

What your clients want is determined by who they are. Who they are is regularly demonstrated by what they do. Think about the clients with whom you do business. Ask yourself: In which of the categories would I place them? What do they do for a living?

If you're working with a mechanical engineer on a labor lawsuit, for example, it's probably safe to assume that he's a neutral client. If another one of your clients is a cardiologist, she's probably tactile. Accountants tend to be traditional and software engineers are often experimental.

Having an idea about which categories your clients may fall into is very helpful to figuring out what they want. Of course, there's no exact science to it, and human beings constantly defy stereotypes. So don't take my word for it. You'll want to make your own analysis of the clients you serve.

Confusion 2: How to Communicate Effectively with Your Client

The next step in the client satisfaction process is to decide how to magnify the characteristics of your practice that are most likely to appeal to your preferred category of client. That begins with what marketing people call your *positioning strategy*.

What do I mean by *positioning* your practice? You position your practice with words. A few well-chosen words to tell your clients exactly what they want to hear. In marketing lingo, those words are called your USP, or unique selling proposition.

For example, if you are targeting tactile clients (ones who love people), your USP could be: "Timothy Thompson Law Offices, where the feelings of people *really* count!" This might be particularly effective for a practice that focuses on family law or other emotionally charged legal issues.

If you are targeting experimental clients (ones who love new, revolutionary things), your USP could be: "Timothy Thompson Law Offices, where living on the edge is a way of life!" In other words, when they choose to hire someone from your practice, they can count on your legal services being unique, original, and on the cutting edge.

Is this starting to make sense? Do you see how the ordinary things most attorneys do to get clients can be done in a significantly more effective way?

Once you understand the essential principles of marketing the E-Myth way, the strategies by which you attract clients can make an enormous difference in your market share.

Confusion 3: How to Keep Your Client Happy

Let's say you've overcome the first two confusions. Great. Now how do you keep your client happy? Very simple: Just keep your promise! And make sure that your client *knows* you kept your promise every step of the way.

In short, giving your clients what they think they want is the key to keeping your clients (or anyone else, for that matter) really happy.

If your clients need to interact with people (high touch, tactile), make certain that they do.

If they need to interact with things (high-tech, neutral), make certain that they do.

If they need to interact with ideas (in their head, withdrawal), make certain that they do.

And so forth.

At E-Myth, we call this your *client fulfillment system*. It's the step-by-step process by which you do the task you've contracted to do and deliver what you've promised—on time, every time.

But what happens when your clients are *not* happy? What happens when you've done everything I've mentioned here and your client is still dissatisfied?

Confusion 4: How to Deal with Client Dissatisfaction

If you have followed each step up to this point, client dissatisfaction will be rare. But it can and will still occur—people are people, and some people will always find a way to be dissatisfied with something. Here's what to do about it:

1. Always listen to what your clients are saying. And never interrupt while they're saying it.

2. After you're sure that you've heard all of your client's complaint, make absolutely certain you understand what she said by phrasing a question, such as: "Can I repeat what you've just told me, Ms. Ancona, to make absolutely certain I understand you?"

3. Secure your client's acknowledgement that you have heard her complaint accurately.

4. Apologize for whatever your client thinks you did that dissatisfied her, even if you didn't do it!

5. After your client has acknowledged your apology, ask her exactly what would make her happy.

6. Repeat what your client told you would make her happy, and get her acknowledgement that you have heard correctly.

7. If at all possible, give your client exactly what she has asked for.

You may be thinking, "But what if my client wants something totally impossible? Or even illegal?"

Don't worry. If you've followed my recommendations to the letter, what your client asks for will seldom seem unreasonable. And they will cease asking you to violate your ethical canons or the law itself. Or they'll go to some other attorney when they want to play fast and loose with the law.

Confusion 5: Whom to Call a Client

At this stage, it's important to ask yourself some questions about the kind of clients you hope to attract to your practice:

- Which types of clients would you most like to do business with?
- Where do you see your real market opportunities?
- Who would you like to work with, provide legal services to, and position your business for?

To what category of client are you most drawn? A tactile client for whom people are most important? A neutral client for whom the mechanics of how you practice law is most important? An experimental client for whom cutting-edge innovation is important? A traditional client for whom low cost and certainty of delivery are absolutely essential?

Once you've defined your ideal clients, go after them. There's no reason you can't attract these types of people to your legal practice and give them exactly what they want.

In short, *it's all up to you.* No mystery. No magic. Just a systematic process for shaping your practice's future. But you must have the passion to pursue the process. And you must be absolutely clear about every aspect of it.

Until you know your clients as well as you know yourself.

Until all your complaints about clients are a thing of the past.

Until you accept the undeniable fact that client acquisition and client satisfaction are more science than art.

But unless you're willing to grow your practice, you better not follow any of these recommendations. Because if you do what I'm suggesting, it's going to grow.

This brings us to the subject of *growth*. But first, let's listen to what Robert and Sandy have to say about clients.

www.michaelegerber.com/attorney

Your Client Loves You, He Loves You Not

Robert Armstrong
Sanford M. Fisch

The glue that holds all relationships together—including the relationship between the leader and the led, is trust. And trust is based on integrity.
—Brian Tracy

The relationship between the attorney and her or his client is a peculiar thing. The client is entrusting you to handle some of his most important affairs, yet may not trust you to present him with an honest bill.

Likewise, your client is the lifeline of your firm, yet that same client is also often the most annoying thorn in your side. Now if that's not a love/hate relationship, I don't know what is!

But what's really interesting is not that this relationship exists, but that both parties seem content in allowing it to continue in its current state. I mean, let's be honest here: When was the last time you gave any real effort to improving your relationships with existing clients?

If the answer doesn't immediately come to you, you're not alone. When most attorneys talk about building their practices, they frequently focus on attracting new clientele. They believe that as long as their marketing efforts provide a steady stream of new clients, their businesses will grow and thrive. But limiting your client development activities to finding and engaging new clients is a huge mistake.

And that's why for years, we've encouraged lawyers to abandon the mind-set that clients are a one-time transaction, and substitute it with the notion that each client has a lifetime value.

Of course, you'll certainly want to continue to bring new clients into your firm—that's just good business. But a large chunk of your client development budget should be spent on retention of existing clients, not attracting new ones. And here's why:

- The costs of attracting a new client are 5 to 12 times greater than the cost of retaining an existing client.
- The return on investment (ROI) for client retention activities is 10 times higher than for new client marketing.
- Existing clients can be the best source of new client referrals, out-producing even the best marketing efforts.
- Leveraging the potential of existing clients quickly increases bottom-line profits.

Make no mistake: The best tool for attracting new business is your existing client base. Trouble is, in the typical law firm, the importance of existing clients is frequently underestimated or overlooked altogether.

All too often, attorneys pin their hopes of building a successful business on expensive marketing campaigns, while ignoring, in the words of Russell Conwell, "the acres of diamonds" that surround them.

Here's an exercise that will help you understand the value of what we're advocating. Take a look at your roster of established clients and ask yourself: What additional services will each client likely need in the future? What are the possible referral sources? To which groups or centers of influence could each client introduce me? Calculate the potential revenue from each existing client. You'll be amazed to discover the value of your "acres of diamonds."

As an example of those acres, we recently helped one estate planning attorney recognize that his average client was worth more than $25,000 in additional business over the course of a lifetime. This means you can think of a client's value to your business in the short term by looking only at the value of the immediate services that you provide, or you can choose to focus on the lifetime value of the client. It's your choice. But we suggest you change your perspective so that you can be rewarded handsomely.

Changing how you value clients will alter the entire dynamic of your relationship and reshape your marketing endeavors. For example, how much would you pay in client acquisition costs to acquire a new client where the transaction was $3,500 versus $25,000?

Our view is that you don't get a client to make a sale but instead, make a sale to get a client. Once the initial contact has been made, it is your job as the attorney to nurture and develop a solid, sustainable relationship with the client. And to do that, you need only remember one thing: It doesn't matter what you want—it's what the client wants that counts.

Fortunately, figuring out what your clients want isn't as hard as you might think. For starters, they want to be heard. They want a little understanding, maybe some compassion and even empathy for their current situation. They want to feel that you appreciate their business and that you respect them as human beings. Oh, and they'd also like to trust that your legal expertise can help solve their problems. That's not too much to ask, is it?

In a law office that's primarily concerned with billable hours, yes, it probably is too much to ask. But in your firm, your "revolutionary" firm, this type of service should be the norm.

Of course, you'll need systems in place to ensure that's the case because sadly, more than 90% of your dissatisfied clients will simply never return, and they won't tell you why they left. They will, however, tell others—every chance they get.

In fact, customer satisfaction studies continue to report that each dissatisfied client will tell between ten and twenty people about their bad experience. That's ten to twenty potential new clients that you'll never see. But keep your clients happy and you'll reap the benefits of the same word-of-mouth network that could have quickly tanked your reputation.

That means new clients for your firm without spending a marketing penny. How's that for efficiency?

Now, the good news is that keeping your clients happy is relatively easy in most cases. Simply maintaining regular communication can go a long way in fostering client satisfaction. Throw in some honesty and integrity and you've got yourself a winning combination. After all, it's much harder to sue someone for malpractice when that person continuously goes the extra mile for you, whether they made a mistake or not.

If you sincerely want to build a law business that will last for the long term, you must have a system in place that attracts new clients to your roster while providing continued service to your existing book of business. This is the only way to build the kind of client loyalty that leads to an inexhaustible source of referrals.

This system begins with communication. Regular contact with all your clients is essential. Start with systematic contact several times a year and build on that. We recommend touching base at least once a month.

And don't be boring about it. Look for creative and interesting ways to communicate, such as client newsletters, greeting cards for birthdays, anniversaries, holidays—you get the idea. Plan special client appreciation events like ice cream socials or an open house. Take your clients bowling, throw a dance in their honor, make it fun.

Your clients want to bond with you and your firm. They want to see you as people, not faceless professionals. Many attorneys think that it diminishes their credibility to be "people" rather than professionals, but the only way to build trust is to let your clients get to know who you are. You don't have to be the stuffy, distant, and arrogant attorney in order to impress people and get business. In fact, it's a myth that's costing you revenue.

And since we're talking about talking, communication with your clients shouldn't be exclusively about the law. Talk about yourself, your hobbies, your vacations, or even funny incidents that happen to you or your staff.

Yes, your clients want to know what's going on in their case but beyond that, your communications can be more casual. They already know that you're competent—if they didn't, you wouldn't be their attorney. What they need now is to see that you're human—that you have a dog or like to run or volunteer once a month at the local shelter.

These are the qualities that draw people to you, not your prestigious degrees and awards. And if you doubt this theory, then think about your doctor. Despite all his or her medical expertise, if their bedside manner is lacking, you won't hesitate to find someone else.

Don't you suppose the attorney–client relationship works the same way? Here's a test. If you have a newsletter that you send to clients, insert an article about your dog, your vacation, an achievement of your kids, something memorable about your staff, and track what items your clients talk about. We guarantee the next time they come in or call you on the phone they will comment about your vacation, your dog, or that funny incident in the office well before they mention the new tax law that you wrote about extensively. Communicating systematically in this way will be enormously rewarding. You'll own the field in your community, because everyone else is still living in the dark ages.

Remember, the value of your business is determined by your clients, your connection to them, and most importantly the systems you have in place to continue and enhance those relationships. Look at how you can improve both the initial contact with each client as well as their subsequent interactions to ensure they always feel connected, cared about, and important to the firm.

Superior client fulfillment based on a tight system will lead to continuing client satisfaction, not to mention that it will generate a few referrals in the process. The result of all of this will be consistent, sustainable growth, bringing you one very big step closer to your vision of what a law practice should be.

www.michaelegerber.com/attorney

On the Subject of Growth

Michael E. Gerber

In studying the history of the human mind one is impressed again and again by the fact that the growth of the mind is the widening of the range of consciousness, and that each step forward has been a most painful and laborious achievement.

—Carl Jung

The rule of business growth says that every business, like every child, is destined to grow. Needs to grow. Is determined to grow.

Once you've created your legal practice, once you've shaped the idea of it, the most natural thing for it to do is to . . . *grow*! And if you stop it from growing, it will die.

Once an attorney has started a practice, it's his or her job to help it grow. To nurture it and support it in every way. To infuse it with:

- Purpose
- Passion
- Will

- Belief
- Personality
- Method

As your practice grows, it naturally changes. And as it changes from a little practice to something much bigger, you will begin to feel out of control. And that's because you *are* out of control!

Your practice *has* exceeded your know-how, sprinted right past you, and now it's taunting you to keep up. That leaves you two choices: Grow as big as your practice demands you grow, or try to hold your practice at its present level—at the level you feel most comfortable.

The sad fact is that most attorneys do the latter. They try to keep their practice small, securely within their comfort zone. Doing what they know how to do, what they feel most comfortable doing. It's called playing it safe.

But as the practice grows, the number, scale, and complexity of tasks will grow, too, until they threaten to overwhelm the attorney. More people are needed. More space. More money. Everything seems to be happening at the same time. A hundred balls are in the air at once.

As I've said throughout this book: *Most attorneys are not entrepreneurs. They aren't true businesspeople at all, but technicians suffering from an entrepreneurial seizure.* Their philosophy of coping with the workload can be summarized as "just do it," rather than figuring out how to get it done through other people using innovative systems to produce consistent results.

Given most attorneys' inclination to be the master juggler in their practice, it's not surprising that as complexity increases, as work expands beyond their ability to do it, as money becomes more elusive, they are just holding on, desperately juggling more and more balls. In the end, most collapse under the strain.

You can't expect your practice to stand still. You can't expect your practice to stay small. A practice that stays small and depends on you to do everything isn't a practice—it's a job!

Yes, just like your children, your business must be allowed to grow, to flourish, to change, to become more than it is. In this way, it will match your vision.

Do you feel the excitement? You should. After all, you know what your practice *is* but not what it *can be*.

It's either going to grow or die. The choice is yours, but it is a choice that must be made. If you sit back and wait for change to overtake you, you will always have to answer "no" to this question: Are you ready?

This brings us to the subject of *change*. But first, let's listen to what Robert and Sandy have to say about growth.

www.michaelegerber.com/attorney

CHAPTER

18

Growth

Robert Armstrong
Sanford M. Fisch

If you don't know where you're going, you'll probably end up some-where else.

—Yogi Berra

I t is the nature of any business to grow. First one client and then another, new projects come along and new ideas are born. And slowly but surely, the business begins to expand. The systems and processes we've discussed in previous chapters are designed to help you grow effortlessly and efficiently, but make no mistake, your business *will* grow, whether you're ready for it or not.

And since you're reading this book, my guess is that you've come to that fork in the road. Your business is ready to grow—are you ready to grow with it?

Assuming that your answer is "yes," then it's time for you to make that leap and change the way you see your firm. A well-run legal practice on a fast track for growth must exist as a separate entity from its attorney-owner. Although you the owner may work in the business with clearly defined tasks, the practice itself is your creation, one with a life of its own. Like a machine designed by an engineer or a house built by an architect, the practice itself is *the product* to be shaped and molded and should be able to "stand" whether you're around to run it or not.

Unfortunately, this is not the case with most practices we see. They are neither created nor operated as businesses, but revolve completely around the personality and capacity limits of the attorney. If the lawyer stops working, takes a vacation, or heaven forbid, wants to retire some day, the practice revenue stops too. Sadly, in the real world there's very little difference between a regular lawyer with a job and the owner of a law practice.

Which brings us back to that fork in the road: The old way of doing things just simply won't work anymore. As the way we live and work continues to evolve, so must your law firm.

Lincoln once said, "A lawyer's time and advice are his stock in trade," but that's no longer completely true. The billable hour is giving way to alternative methods like the flat-fee model. Staffing is being leveraged so that paralegals and other paraprofessionals are taking over as many duties in the firm as possible, allowing the attorney to spend more time developing business strategies and doing the work that only a licensed attorney can do.

But it's not just fee models and staffing that are changing. Leveraging the work product through automation is finally being accepted by a profession that is known for its risk-adverse attitude toward technology, which is embedded in its soul as deeply as its affinity for footnotes. And for good reason: Like any business, time is money to the legal profession. The more time it takes to perform routine tasks, the greater the cost to the firm. Reducing the time it takes to perform routine tasks saves money and frees up time to perform additional tasks thereby creating an opportunity to generate even more revenue.

Utilizing technology means upgrading computer hardware and finding time-saving software applications to make work more efficient. It can mean outsourcing business tasks to experts or lower-wage workers for routine tasks. It means looking at new marketing opportunities in the online world. It means embracing the web with an interactive web site that provides quality content and answers to all those commonly asked questions.

It means looking at creating visibility with a blog that shares your wisdom and allows people to see who you are and what you have to offer. It may mean using new online advertising methods like Google AdWords to generate clients. Social media sites like Facebook, Twitter, LinkedIn, and AVVO are opening up a new world for attorneys to maintain relationships with existing clients, referral sources, attract new clients, and grow. These are new models that give us a glimpse of what the future of legal services may look like.

We are the beneficiaries of the greatest technological revolution this world has ever seen. Ignore the transformational changes that are occurring all around you, and your practice will wither and die. Old-school thinking argues that it shouldn't be this way, but it is; that attorneys and clients should continue to adhere to a process that was established years ago, but they won't. A new day has dawned. Technology today provides sophisticated and efficient ways of completing routine tasks, tracking client matters, generating custom documents, collaborating online, and communicating the results instantly. With the rise of the personal and networked computer and the growth of the Internet, you would think every attorney in practice today would embrace this new way of doing business, but sadly it's not true.

When we do technology audits on firms we work with, we're shocked to see the antiquated technology systems in play. Other than the biggest firms, very few practices have comprehensive accounting and billing systems, document-generating software, or relational databases to track everything. Instead, yellow legal pads, a rolodex, giant day planners, and bulging manila folders are the currency of most firms. As a result, a regular law firm scene is a staff person scurrying from office to office asking if anyone has seen the Johnson file.

By the dawn of the twenty-first century, new digital technology made it possible for law firms and legal professionals to engage in the practice of law via cyberspace. This new practice approach known as eLawyering utilizes the Internet and cloud computing for the direct delivery of legal services. The market is huge. Research shows that the next generation of clients is much more comfortable interacting online with minimal face-to-face contact and very little of the traditional hand-holding of the more traditional legal practice model. They are often willing to make large financial transactions without ever meeting anyone face-to-face. We recently spoke with an attorney who was offering a package of legal consulting services for $7,500 online and most people had no problem placing the full sum on their credit card without ever having any more than a cyber-relationship.

At a recent national conference, a speaker from the ABA task force on eLawyering made a persuasive case that there is a huge underserved market that is wary of lawyers and their fees. He talked about new ways to deliver services to the more Internet-literate population who are comfortable conducting business online. The talk was very controversial, with the audience dividing itself into three basic groups: The *early adopters* wanted to sign up right away, the *skeptics* wanted to wait and see how things worked out, and the *naysayers* thought eLawyering should be outlawed.

As the ABA has pointed out in recent publications, the practice of law over the Internet doesn't come without "far reaching implications for the legal profession that go beyond the use of personal computers on the desktop." One of the major concerns is that the shift of a legal practice to a digital platform presents ethical dilemmas that involve a wide variety of issues, including confidentiality and communication with prospective clients. Yet to be addressed are the challenges involved in the multijurisdictional practice of law and the threat to local and state bar regulators across the country.

We don't have all the answers to the issues regarding eLawyering, but we are confident that the demands of the consumer will cause these issues to eventually be resolved. One thing remains clear: The power of innovation must permeate the law firm that is going to grow. Peter Drucker famously said that there are only two aspects to any successful business, innovation and marketing, both of which will inevitably lead to growth.

But the sad fact is that most lawyers we come in contact with don't even own basic contact-management software that holds client information, and tracks all communications with staff, clients, and vendors; or software that can generate marketing reports and deliver an instant dashboard of the vital signs of the business.

This kind of technology provides the tools that will keep you on the fast track to growth. Leveraging these tools, plus systems and trained support staff can guarantee that the firm will not be caught by surprise when conditions change.

With times rapidly changing, lawyers with traditional skills and attitudes are on shaky ground in this new emerging economy. The ones who could imagine a better way to acquire clients and deliver legal services are the new stars. Thomas Friedman, the bestselling author and *New York Times* columnist illustrated this point perfectly.

"A Washington lawyer friend recently told me about layoffs at his firm. I asked him who was getting axed. He said it was interesting: lawyers who were used to just showing up and having work handed to them were the first to go because with the bursting of the credit bubble, that flow of work just isn't there. But those who have the ability to imagine new services, new opportunities and new ways to recruit work were being retained. They are the new *untouchables*."

Just being an average accountant, lawyer, contractor, or assembly-line worker is not the ticket it used to be. As Daniel Pink, the author of *A Whole New Mind*, puts it: In a world in which more and more average work can be done by a computer, robot or talented foreigner faster, cheaper 'and just as well,' vanilla doesn't cut it anymore."

We believe and teach that the practice of law is a business, and that in a business there is no "status quo." You are either winning or losing; things are either getting better or getting worse. Like life itself, you are either growing or decaying.

Trouble is, most attorneys don't have their finger on the pulse of their businesses. They are too busy "working in the business" on tactical tasks instead of "working on the business" engaged in strategic work. Too often the result is that they discover too late that their business is dying.

There simply is no substitute for having systems in place that provide the kinds of critical information you need on things like marketing activity, conversion to clients, legal work produced and status, and financial information. The key to a successful, growing practice is to be eternally vigilant. Pay attention to details, regularly examine the information provided by your systems, and then adjust whenever and wherever it becomes necessary.

You must know where you're going. And to get there, your goal must be to go from a practice that is dependent upon you, to a business you run.

Up to this point, we've certainly covered a lot of ground. We've tried to lay out a vision that will transform your practice into a real business. So our question for you, and one that we have asked attorneys at workshops for years, is what is preventing you from taking decisive action to reengineer your law firm, and by extension, your life?

We've heard all the different answers but the truth is, you stare at the biggest barrier to your own success in the mirror every day. It's not a surprise, is it? As attorneys we have been trained to see only the issues and problems, that is, why things can't work. We call this the "lawyer trap." It's where you tell yourself every reason why this won't work for you or your practice. Your firm is too big. It's too small. You live in a rural area. You live in an urban setting. You're too old. You're too young. You get the idea. We've heard all the reasons why. Chances are if you've made it this far, you may be able to get a glimpse of what possibilities are just around the corner. Hold on to those dreams and imagine, with a little action, what your law firm could become. Remember, any real change in life always starts with a decision.

www.michaelegerber.com/attorney

On the Subject of Change

Michael E. Gerber

What happens is not as important as how you react to what happens.
—Thaddeus Golas

So your practice is growing. That means, of course, that it's also changing. Which means it's driving you and everyone in your life crazy.

That's because, to most people, change is a diabolical thing. Tell most people they've got to change, and they will crawl into a shell. Nothing threatens their existence more than change. Nothing cements their resistance more than change. Nothing.

Yet for the past 35 years, that's exactly what I've been proposing to small business owners: the need to change. Not for the sake of change, but for the sake of their lives.

I've talked to countless attorneys whose hopes weren't being realized through their practice; whose lives were consumed by work; who slaved increasingly longer hours for decreasing pay; whose dissatisfaction grew as their enjoyment shriveled; whose practice had become the worst job in the world; whose money was out of control; and whose employees, both attorneys and support staff, were a source of never-ending hassles, just like their clients, their bank, and, increasingly, even their family.

More and more, these attorneys spent their time alone, dreading the unknown and anxious about their future. And even when they were with people, they didn't know how to relax. Their mind was always on the job. They were distracted by work, by the thought of work. By the fear of falling behind.

And yet, when confronted with their condition and offered an alternative, most of the same attorneys strenuously resisted. They assumed that if there were a better way of doing business, they already would have figured it out. They derived comfort from knowing what they believed they already knew. They accepted the limitations of being an attorney; or the truth about people; or the limitations of what they could expect from their clients, their employees, their associate lawyers, their bankers—even their family and friends.

In short, most attorneys I've met over the years would rather live with the frustrations they already have than risk enduring new frustrations.

Isn't that true of most people you know? Rather than opening up to the infinite number of possibilities life offers, they prefer to shut their life down to respectable limits. After all, isn't that the most reasonable way to live?

I think not. I think we must learn to let go. I think that if you fail to embrace change, it will inevitably destroy you. Conversely, by opening yourself to change, you give your legal practice the opportunity to get the most from your talents.

Let me share with you an original way to think about change, about life, about who we are and what we do. About the stunning notion of expansion and contraction.

Contraction versus Expansion

"Our salvation," a wise man once said, "is to allow." That is, to be open, to let go of our beliefs, to change. Only then can we move from a point of view to a viewing point.

That wise man was Thaddeus Golas, the author of a small, powerful book entitled, *The Lazy Man's Guide to Enlightenment* (Seed Center, 1971).

Among the many inspirational things he had to say was this compelling idea:

> The basic function of each being is expanding and contracting. Expanded beings are permeative; contracted beings are dense and impermeative. Therefore each of us, alone or in combination, may appear as space, energy, or mass, depending on the ration of expansion to contraction chosen, and what kind of vibrations each of us expresses by alternating expansion and contraction. Each being controls his own vibrations.

In other words, Golas tells us that the entire mystery of life can be summed up in two words: *expansion* and *contraction*. He goes on to say:

> We experience expansion as awareness, comprehension, understanding, or whatever we wish to call it.

When we are completely expanded, we have a feeling of total awareness, of being one with all life. At that level we have no resistance to any vibrations or interactions with other beings. It is timeless bliss, with unlimited choice of consciousness, perception, and feeling.

On the other hand, when a (human) being is totally contracted, he is a mass particle, completely imploded. To the degree that he is contracted, a being is unable to be in the same space with others, so contraction is felt as fear, pain, unconsciousness, ignorance, hatred, evil, and a whole host of strange feelings.

At an extreme (of contraction), a human being has the feeling of being completely insane, of resisting everyone and everything, of being unable to choose the content of his consciousness.

Of course, these are just the feelings appropriate to mass vibration levels, and he can get out of them at any time by expanding, by letting go of all resistance to what he thinks, sees, or feels.

Stay with me here. Because what Golas says is profoundly important. When you're feeling oppressed, overwhelmed, exhausted by more than you can control—contracted, as Golas puts it—you can change your state to one of expansion.

According to Golas, the more contracted we are, the more threatened by change; the more expanded we are, the more open to change. In our most enlightened—that is, open—state, change is as welcome as non-change. Everything is perceived as a part of ourselves. There is no inside or outside. Everything is one thing. Our sense of isolation is transformed to a feeling of ease, of light, of joyful relationship with everything.

As infants, we didn't even think of change in the same way, because we lived those first days in an unthreatened state. Insensitive to the threat of loss, most young children are only aware of *what is*. Change is simply another form of *what is*. Change just *is*.

However, when we are in our most contracted—that is, closed—state, change is the most extreme threat. If the known is what I have, then the unknown must be what threatens to take away what I have. Change, then, is the unknown. And the unknown is fear. It's like being between trapezes.

To the fearful, change is threatening because things may get worse.

To the hopeful, change is encouraging because things may get better.

To the confident, change is inspiring because the challenge exists to improve things.

If you are fearful, you see difficulties in every opportunity. If you are fear-free, you see opportunities in every difficulty.

Fear protects what I have from being taken away. But it also disconnects me from the rest of the world. In other words, fear keeps me separate and alone.

Here's the exciting part of Golas's message: With this new understanding of contraction and expansion, we can become completely attuned to where we are at all times.

If I am afraid, suspicious, skeptical, and resistant, I am in a contracted state. If I am joyful, open, interested, and willing, I am in an expanded state. Just knowing this puts me on an expanded path. Always remembering this, Golas says, brings enlightenment, which opens me even more.

Such openness gives me the ability to freely access my options. And taking advantage of options is the best part of change. Just as there are infinite ways to win a case, there are infinite ways to run your practice. If you believe Thaddeus Golas, your most exciting option is to be open to all of them.

Because your life is lived on a continuum between the most contracted and most expanded—the most closed and most open—states, change is best understood as the movement from one to the other, and back again.

Most small business owners I've met see change as a thing-in-itself, as something that just happens to them. Most experience change as a threat. Whenever change shows up at the door, they quickly slam it. Many bolt the door and pile up the furniture. Some even run for their gun.

Few of them understand that change isn't a thing-in-itself, but rather the manifestation of many things. You might call it the revelation of all possibilities. Think of it as the ability at any moment to sacrifice what we are for what we could become.

Change can either challenge us or threaten us. It's our choice. Our attitude toward change can either pave the way to success or throw up a roadblock.

Change is where opportunity lives. Without change we would stay exactly as we are. The universe would be frozen still. Time would end.

At any given moment, we are somewhere on the path between a contracted and expanded state. Most of us are in the middle of the journey, neither totally closed nor totally open. According to Golas, change is our movement from one place in the middle toward one of the two ends.

Do you want to move toward contraction or toward enlightenment? Because without change, you are hopelessly stuck with what you've got.

Without change:

- We have no hope.
- We cannot know true joy.
- We will not get better.
- We will continue to focus exclusively on what we have and the threat of losing it.

All of this negativity contracts us even more, until, at the extreme closed end of the spectrum, we become a black hole so dense that no light can get in or out.

Sadly, the harder we try to hold on to what we've got, the less able we are to do so. So we try still harder, which eventually drags us even deeper into the black hole of contraction.

Are you like that? Do you know anybody who is?

Think of change as the movement between where we are and where we're not. That leaves only two directions for change: either moving forward or slipping backward. We either become more contracted or more expanded.

The next step is to link change to how we feel. If we feel afraid, change is dragging us backward. If we feel open, change is pushing us forward.

Change is not a thing-in-itself, but a movement of our consciousness. By tuning in, by paying attention, we get clues to the state of our being.

Change, then, is not an outcome or something to be acquired. Change is a shift of our consciousness, of our being, of our humanity, of our attention, of our relationship with all other beings in the universe.

We are either "more in relationship" or "less in relationship." Change is the movement in either of those directions. The exciting part is that *we possess the ability to decide which way we go . . . and to know in the moment which way we're moving.*

Closed, open. . . . Open, closed. Two directions in the universe. The choice is yours.

Do you see the profound opportunity available to you? What an extraordinary way to live!

Enlightenment is not reserved for the sainted. Rather, it comes to us as we become more sensitive to ourselves. Eventually, we become our own guides, alerting ourselves to our state, moment by moment: *open . . . closed . . . open . . . closed.*

Listen to your inner voice, your ally, and feel what it's like to be open and closed. Experience the instant of choice in both directions.

You will feel the awareness growing. It may be only a flash at first, so be alert. This feeling is accessible, but only if you avoid the black hole of contraction.

Are you afraid that you're totally contracted? Don't be—it's doubtful. The fact that you're still reading this book suggests that you're moving in the opposite direction.

You're more like a running back seeking the open field. You can see the opportunity gleaming in the distance. In the open direction.

Understand that I'm not saying that change itself is a point on the path; rather, it's the all-important movement.

Change is *in you*, not *out there*.

What path are you on? The path of liberation? Or the path of crystallization?

As we know, change can be for the better or for the worse. If change is happening *inside* of you, it is for the worse only if you remain closed to it. The key, then, is your attitude—your acceptance or rejection of change. Change can be for the better only if you accept it. And it will certainly be for the worse if you don't.

Remember, change is nothing in itself. Without you, change doesn't exist. Change is happening inside of each of us, giving us clues to where we are at any point in time. Rejoice in change, for it's a sign you are alive.

Are we open? Are we closed? If we're open, good things are bound to happen. If we're closed, things will only get worse. According to Golas, it's as simple as that. Whatever happens defines where we are. *How* we are is *where* we are. It cannot be any other way.

For change is life. Charles Darwin wrote, "It is not the strongest of the species that survive, nor the most intelligent, but the one that proves itself most responsive to change."

The growth of your legal practice, then, is its change. Your role is to go with it, to be with it, to share the joy, embrace the opportunities, meet the challenges, learn the lessons.

Remember, there are three kinds of people: (1) those who make things happen, (2) those who let things happen, and (3) those who wonder what the hell happened. The people who make things happen are masters of change. The other two are its victims.

Which type are you?

The Big Change

If all this is going to mean anything to the life of your practice, you have to know when you're going to leave it. At what point, in your practice's rise from where it is now to where it can ultimately grow, are you going to sell it? Because if you don't have a clear picture of when you want out, your practice is the master of your destiny, not the reverse.

As we stated earlier, the most valuable form of money is equity, and unless your business vision includes your equity and how you will use it to your advantage, you will forever be consumed by your practice.

Your practice is potentially the best friend you ever had. It is your practice's nature to serve you, so let it. If, however, you are not a wise steward, if you do not tell your practice what you expect from it, it will run rampant, abuse you, use you, and confuse you.

Change. Growth. Equity.

Focus on the point in the future when you will take leave of your practice. Now reconsider your goals in that context. Be specific. Write them down.

Skipping this step is like tiptoeing through earthquake country. Who can say where the fault lies waiting? And who knows exactly when your whole world may come crashing down around you?

Former General Electric CEO Jack Welch famously said that we must all eat change for breakfast. From this day forward, don't skip your breakfast.

Which brings us to the subject of *time*. But first, let's listen to what Robert and Sandy have to say about change.

www.michaelegerber.com/attorney

CHAPTER
20

The Gift of Change

Robert Armstrong
Sanford M. Fisch

When you are through changing, you are through.

—Bruce Barton

I n his book *The End of Lawyers? Rethinking the Nature of Legal Services*, author Richard Susskind discusses the radical changes that will envelop the practice of law during the next ten years. Envisioning the impact of technology and how it will change the function of the attorney, Susskind concludes that for the conservative legal adviser, the future is bleak; but for the progressive lawyer, exciting new markets will emerge.

We tend to agree. In fact, the legal profession has never looked more different than it does today and quite honestly, what we're seeing now is just the tip of the iceberg.

Where you once needed an attorney, now you just need the Internet and a printer, but buyer beware. Online legal documents have streamlined a number of practice areas, offering consumers a seemingly perfectly-crafted, fill-in-the-blank legal document with just a click of the mouse. From wills, trusts, and divorce agreements to sample pleadings, patents, trademarks, contracts, and much more, it's online and it doesn't cost even a fraction of what a consumer would pay you—in fact, it often doesn't cost anything at all.

What's really sad about this new trend is that lawyers have been completely cut out of the deal, the consumers are being hoodwinked, and it's only going to get worse. Travel agents, accountants, and even bank tellers have fallen prey to our technology-driven society. We've replaced face-to-face contact with online banking, virtual shopping carts, and tax preparation software, all of which are open 24/7 and you don't need an appointment to get started.

Booksellers now have to compete with handheld digital book readers that can download that newest bestseller for you in less than a minute, and real estate agents get to compete with online databases that can filter, categorize, compare, and show any property in any state at any time. Honestly, what made us think the legal profession would be safe?

The technology facilitating these changes continues to plow forward, evolving and growing into something bigger and more magnificent than we ever imagined. And while it was once fairly easy to deny the lasting power and effectiveness of computers as another passing fad, that day is long gone and it's time to face the music: The technology is here and it won't be going away.

What's more, it's changing the way we practice law. Yet in the face of all this change, we are incredibly optimistic about the future.

Because "change" means opportunity. Opportunity to grow, to learn, to achieve something that perhaps you hadn't envisioned before. To take advantage of these opportunities, of course, you'll need to be open to the changes that are coming, changes that will require you to rethink the way you approach your practice. Exciting, isn't it?

See, you have a unique advantage that other industries didn't have—not only do you know the changes are coming, but you can also see how they will likely play out. This knowledge puts you in the very coveted position of being able to lead the change rather than just follow along with everyone else.

And isn't that really what you wanted for your practice? To be the firm that set the pace, while your competitors try to keep up?

To make this transformation, you'll need to wear a new hat, one of a visionary that is no longer constrained by the law firm stereotypes we're leaving behind.

Instead of looking for ways to increase your billable hours, look for ways to increase the value you offer to clients. For example, replace your old static web site (assuming you have one), with something that's interactive, engaging, and informative. Don't just recite the credentials of your staff—instead, give answers to commonly asked questions. Explain the differences between mediation and a collaborative divorce, for instance, or list the criteria for creating a valid prenup.

Include a blog that not only highlights the achievements of your firm but also explains recent changes in the law—in layman's terms no less, so that someone looking for this information feels that they "got what they needed" from your site.

Want to combat all those online do-it-yourself forms? Explain why these forms aren't appropriate for certain situations, and then offer package alternatives (we discussed this earlier, remember?) that are priced reasonably enough to make it worth consumers' consideration.

After all, if they were willing to purchase an online form that offered no professional assistance, don't you think they'd be willing to pay a small amount of money for a similar form that came with a once-over or consultation from someone who knows what they're doing?

Be the firm that redefines how a law firm should be. Create brochures that enable clients to come "prepared" for your meeting and send these out with a letter confirming their next appointment.

Have preprinted packages that cover common concerns in your area of practice and give these to clients when the meeting is over. Include CDs or pamphlets and perhaps even a small gift card to your local coffee shop so that clients can go out afterward and discuss the ideas you've presented to them.

Build relationships by continuing to touch base with both prospects and clients, offering new services and packages that reflect not just what you're willing to sell but that also address what the client actually wants to buy. Does this mean the days of big money fees are over? Absolutely not! You can still be the Ritz-Carlton of law firms. In fact, that's exactly what we want you to be.

But remember, what makes the Ritz "The Ritz" is not its hefty price but the service-rich experience you have when you stay there. Mints on your feather pillows, valet service, car service, fruit baskets, continental breakfast—the list just goes on and on.

No one thinks twice about paying their higher-than-average fee because hey, it's The Ritz. Your law firm should be the same way. Like a four-star hotel, you should wrap your clients in extraordinary service—service that goes beyond the acceptable minimum and sets a new standard for other firms to try and match.

It's not the contract, the estate plan, the pleadings, or the research—it's the unique process that you create in your firm to methodically take a client from where they are to where they want to be in a transformative way. Big money can be charged for this process and believe us when we say that happy clients will be glad to pay your fees.

So, while we're recommending creating packages and flat-fee services that highlight price, we don't want that to be your main focus. Quite the contrary: Minimize the issue of price, and instead emphasize the value of relationship, expertise, and client experience.

This is where the "results in advance" concept can really pay off. Give your prospects a taste of what they're looking for without any risk or cost to them. It could be a free report or an educational seminar or some other service or event that moves them further toward their goal.

Now that we're on a roll, let's not stop here! Revamp your marketing strategy to represent the new and improved firm you're now creating. Build those social media profiles we keep talking about and learn what it means to tweet and post.

Build a Facebook page, update your "status" often, and interact with the rest of the digital world. Use your social media presence to share information, promote your services, and connect with the masses because that's really what the digital age is all about: connecting with the masses, not just an elite few.

Create a newsletter—that can be subscribed to from your web site for free and include a special report as a free gift for subscribing. What kind of special report, you ask? How about "10 Secrets to Effective Estate Planning" or "The Five Essential Things Every Landlord Must Know to Avoid Tenant Lawsuits." The topics are endless—just look at your area of practice and think about what kind of information could be useful.

Learn about Really Simple Syndication (RSS) feeds, search engine optimization, article marketing, and even viral videos to drive traffic to your web site and thus, your firm.

And if you think you'll never master all this new technology, fear not, because there are people out there who are happy to handle this kind of thing for you. Designers, programmers, writers—there are thousands of experienced and knowledgeable professionals who are able and willing to hold your hand and walk you into the digital age.

In fact, you may employ people with some of these talents already and just don't know it. After all, just because you haven't embraced the new technology doesn't mean the members of your staff are living in the dark ages, too. Which means you can leverage your staff or outsource this piece of your marketing puzzle altogether—the choice is up to you.

But either way, you'll be taking a big step in the right direction, positioning your firm to be a leader in the new way of lawyering. You'll be embracing the change before the change leaves you—and your firm—in the dust.

www.michaelegerber.com/attorney

CHAPTER

21

On the Subject of Time

Michael E. Gerber

The leading rule for the lawyer, as for the man of every other calling, is diligence.

Leave nothing for tomorrow which can be done today.

—Abraham Lincoln

Common laments among attorneys are, "I'm running out of time!" "I've got to learn how to manage my time more carefully!"

Of course, they see no real solution to this problem. They're just worrying the subject to death. Singing the attorney's blues.

Some make a real effort to control time. Maybe they go to time management classes, or faithfully try to record their activities during every hour of the day.

But it's hopeless. Even when attorneys work harder, even when they keep precise records of their time, there's always a shortage of it. It's as if they're looking at a square clock in a round universe. Something doesn't fit. The result: The attorney is constantly chasing work, money, life. And as a country song once put it, "I'm always running . . . and always running behind."

The reason is simple. Attorneys don't see time for what it really is. They think of time with a small "t," rather than Time with a capital "T."

Yet Time is simply another word for *your life*. It's your ultimate asset, your gift at birth—and you can spend it any way you want. Do you know how you want to spend it? Do you have a plan?

How do *you* deal with Time? Are you even conscious of it? If you are, I bet you are constantly locked into either the future or the past. Relying on either memory or imagination.

Do you recognize these voices? "Once I get through this, I can have a drink . . . go on a vacation . . . retire." "I remember when I was young and practicing law was satisfying."

As you go to bed at midnight, are you thinking about waking up at 6 A.M. so that you can get to the office by 7 A.M. so that you can be in court by 8 A.M. so that you can go to lunch by noon, because you've got a client consultation at 2 P.M. and two hours of work on the Hanson case that needs to be finished by 5 . . . ?

Most of us are prisoners of the future or the past. While pinballing between the two, we miss the richest moments of our life—the present. Trapped forever in memory or imagination, we are strangers to the here and now. Our future is nothing more than an extension of our past, and the present is merely the background.

It's sobering to think that right now each of us is at a precise spot somewhere between the beginning of our Time (our birth) and the end of our Time (our death). No wonder everyone frets about Time. What really terrifies us is that *we're using up our life and we can't stop it*.

It feels as if we're plummeting toward the end with nothing to break our free fall. Time is out of control! Understandably, this is horrifying, mostly because the real issue is not time with a small "t" but Death with a big "D."

From the depths of our existential anxiety, we try to put Time in a different perspective—all the while pretending we can manage it. We talk about Time as though it were something other than what it is. "Time is money," we announce, as though that explains it.

But what every attorney should know is that Time is life. And Time ends! Life ends!

The big, walloping, irresolvable problem is that *we don't know how much Time we have left.*

Do you feel the fear? Do you want to get over it?

Let's look at Time more seriously.

To fully grasp Time with a capital T, you have to ask the big question: *How do I wish to spend the rest of my Time?*

Because I can assure you that if you don't ask that big Question with a big "Q," you will forever be assailed by the little questions. You'll shrink the whole of your life to *this time* and *next time* and the *last time*—all the while wondering, *What time is it?*

It's like running around the deck of a sinking ship worrying about where you left the keys to your cabin.

You must accept that you have only so much Time; that you're using up that Time second by precious second. And that your Time, your life, is the most valuable asset you have. Of course, you can use your Time any way you want. But unless you choose to use it as richly, as rewardingly, as excitingly, as intelligently, as *intentionally* as possible, you'll squander it and fail to appreciate it.

Indeed, if you are oblivious to the value of your Time, you'll commit the single greatest sin: You will live your life unconscious of its passing you by.

Until you deal with Time with a capital "T," you'll worry about time with a small "t" until you have no Time—or life—left. Then your Time will be history . . . along with your life.

I can anticipate the question: If Time is the problem, why not just take on fewer clients? Well, that's certainly an option, but probably not necessary. I know an attorney with a small practice who sees four times as many clients as the average, yet he and his associates don't work long hours. How is it possible? He has a system. Roughly 50% of what needs to be communicated to clients is "downloaded" to the paralegals and office staff. By using this expert system, the employees can do everything the attorney or his associate lawyers would do—everything that isn't attorney dependent. They can't dispense legal advice, of course, but they can brief clients on many other aspects of the law and the unique challenges of their particular case.

Be versus Do

Remember when we all asked, "What do I want to be when I grow up?" It was one of our biggest concerns as children.

Notice that the question isn't, "What do I want to *do* when I grow up?" It's "What do I want to *be*?"

Shakespeare wrote, "To be or not to be." Not, "To do or not to do."

But when you grow up, people always ask you, "What do you *do*?" How did the question change from *being* to *doing*? How did we miss the critical distinction between the two?

Even as children, we sensed the distinction. The real question we were asking was not what we would end up *doing* when we grew up, but who we would *be*.

We were talking about a *life* choice, not a *work* choice. We instinctively saw it as a matter of how we spend our Time, not what we do *in* time.

Look to children for guidance. I believe that as children we instinctively saw Time as life and tried to use it wisely. As children, we wanted to make a life choice, not a work choice. As children, we didn't know—or care—that work had to be done on time, on budget.

Until you see Time for what it really is—your life span—you will always ask the wrong question.

Until you embrace the whole of your Time and shape it accordingly, you will never be able to fully appreciate the moment.

Until you fully appreciate every second that comprises Time, you will never be sufficiently motivated to live those seconds fully.

Until you're sufficiently motivated to live those seconds fully, you will never see fit to change the way you are. You will never take the quality and sanctity of Time seriously.

And unless you take the sanctity of Time seriously, you will continue to struggle to catch up with something behind you. Your frustrations will mount as you try to snatch the second that just whisked by.

If you constantly fret about time with a small "t," then big-T Time will blow right past you. And you'll miss the whole point, the real truth about Time: You can't manage it; you never could. You can only *live* it.

And so that leaves you with these questions: How do I live my life? How do I give significance to it? How can I be here now, in this moment?

Once you begin to ask these questions, you'll find yourself moving toward a much fuller, richer life. But if you continue to be caught up in the banal work you do every day, you're never going to find the time to take a deep breath, exhale, and be present in the now.

So, let's talk about the subject of *work*. But first, let's listen to what Robert and Sandy have to say about time.

www.michaelegerber.com/attorney

What Time Do You Have?

Robert Armstrong
Sanford M. Fisch

We are what we repeatedly do.

—Aristotle

In 1964, the Rolling Stones recorded two versions of a song that was destined to become a rock classic, "Time Is on My Side," and "Time Is on Your Side." A great song, but neither version is honest. Time is not on your side, or ours.

Michael Gerber teaches a sobering lesson in this chapter when he warns that "time" and "life" are essentially synonymous, and that the "time" you have left is really the "life" you have left. Once you accept that fact, time takes on new significance.

Over the years it has been our experience that most attorneys don't manage their time very well, and don't use it productively. In fact, more often than not, they utilize a "paint-by-numbers" approach to life and are often managed by the events that surround them and the fires they have to put out each day. Time manages them, and they wind up with a nice, but unimaginative picture of a life that followed a well-traveled path, but lacked the magnificence of the masterpiece it could have been.

In the words of Dr. Walter M. Bortz, professor of medicine at Stanford, "we live short and die long," and the urgency of getting on with what we are meant to do with this one short life increases with each passing day.

We're not just talking about professional accomplishments, but rather being the kind of person that you're intended to be in every area of life. We're talking about a life that is rich in a variety of experiences, including helping the kids with their homework, spending quality time with your significant other, caring for elderly parents, driving the school carpool, dealing with chores in the home, and spending time with friends. And the point of it all lies in a fundamental challenge to make our lives themselves a creative work of art.

Our philosophy is centered on a simple, but powerful, technique called "time blocking." Time blocking involves consistently setting aside time for the high-priority activities in both your work and personal life.

After all, let's face it—you cannot be effective in your professional life if your inner reserves are depleted. Periodically, you need to make time to recharge your batteries and give yourself an energy boost. Block time for exercise, meditation, relaxation, or recreation, and don't forget to carve out time for your family and friends. Treat appointments with yourself just as respectfully as you would with others.

At work, block the time you will need to do the work of an attorney/owner. But consider this: Try to schedule a block of time each day to focus on building your business. Use this uninterrupted time to plan or work on special projects, develop marketing plans, train and develop your staff, or simply to learn something new that will help you grow your business. This will yield rich dividends in short order. Just be sure you don't compromise this time with extraneous activities, or surrender it altogether because of the pressures of the moment.

One of the keys to managing your time more effectively is to determine how you are currently spending your time. A time log is an excellent way to do this. We suggest you keep a time log for a week. After trying it, you will immediately gain some important insights about how you could manage your time better. Understanding where you are spending your time is the first step in changing some bad habits.

Here's how to keep a time log. We recommend that throughout each day of your selected week, you record the time whenever you start and stop any activity in which you become involved. Consider logging your time for the entire day, not just your workday. A stopwatch would be a helpful tool in determining the exact amount of time you spend on various activities. Remember to be as detailed as possible. It is not at all unlikely that you will log a hundred entries or more per day.

Once you have collected the data, sort it into general categories (i.e., client meetings, document preparation, email, web surfing, phone calls, administrative tasks, marketing, research, eating, spending time with your significant other, attending meetings, playing with your kids, and yes even going to the bathroom). Calculate the percentage of time you spent in each activity. At the end of the week, determine what percentage of your time is being spent on each activity.

If you're like most of the attorneys we've worked with, you'll find that the biggest time waster of them all is the evil but necessary email. No question that it's an excellent tool when judiciously used, but most lawyers we talk with check their email incessantly all day long on the off chance that they've missed something. Set up a schedule for checking email that only involves a few select times during the day, and let that schedule be widely known. You'll be surprised at how much more you will be able to accomplish, and how little you missed.

Here are a few other suggestions that will help you become more efficient and, as a result, have more time to balance your work with every other part of your life.

- Analyze your time log and determine what you are doing that could be delegated . . . and then delegate it. In addition to your firm's "daily revenue number," that we discussed earlier in this book, we want to introduce you to another important tool—the value of an hour of your time. This will help you determine what work should be handed over to someone else. Essentially, you divide your ideal annual compensation by the number of hours you're available to work. The result represents how much one hour of your time should be worth. If there's anything you're doing that could be delegated for less than your hourly rate, then "delegated" it should be.

- Determine what your highest and best use of your time is—based on your strengths—and see what percentage of your time is actually being spent in this area.

- Develop a plan to make sure everyone around you does not waste your time and then stick to it. Interruptions are common in a law firm, but they can be dramatically reduced by effective staff meetings where questions are raised and answered, rather than asked of the attorney throughout the workday. Properly planned "stand-up meetings" with key staff during the week can also eliminate interruptions and increase productivity.

- You might want to encourage your staff to log their activities for a week as well. They may be surprised to learn how little time they are actually spending on work-related projects. Studies have concluded that the average office worker only performs about 1.5 hours of actual work each day. The balance of their workday is spent socializing, taking coffee breaks, engaging in non–business-related communication, as well as other non-work tasks. (Remember, this is intended to be a lesson in self-discovery, not an opportunity to find fault. Allow staff members to learn from this activity without feeling that they are the subjects of a management time study.)

- One final tip: Do the most important two or three items for the day first thing when you arrive in the office. This alone will revolutionize your productivity.

Now, we know you've heard some of these ideas before, and we also know you probably wrote them off. But before you make that same mistake again, take a hard look at your time log and consider what it's telling you.

The information contained in your time log could be the key to changing the way you experience your day. Like the athlete who reviews a video after a game, your time log allows you to play the part of "spectator" and see where you need work.

Another tool we've found to be useful is the weekly planner form we use at the Academy. Now, if you think you've seen weekly planners before, think again—this is something that will totally revolutionize the way you envision your time.

Not only does it allow you to plan your weekly calendar, but it also ties together all those important components we've been discussing, such as your daily numbers, your strategic projects and even your most critical tasks. The result is that you have everything you need to manage your time efficiently and productively, and it's all in one place.

If you'd like to try our weekly planner form, just visit our web site at www.michaelegerber.com/attorney.

Using tools like these also allow you to ensure that your time—and thus, your life—is being spent the way you want it to be spent. That the things you consider to be your highest priorities are actually getting their due. Because when you put first things first you begin making full use of your greatest asset: the life you have left.

www.michaelegerber.com/attorney

On the Subject of Work

Michael E. Gerber

Perception is strong and sight weak. In strategy it is important to see distant things as if they were close and to take a distanced view of close things.

—Miyamoto Musashi

In the business world, as the saying goes, the entrepreneur knows something about everything, the technician knows everything about something, and the switchboard operator just knows everything.

In a legal practice, attorneys see their natural work as the work of the technician. The supreme technician. Often to the exclusion of everything else.

After all, attorneys get zero preparation working as a manager and spend no time thinking as an entrepreneur—those just aren't courses offered in law school. By the time they own their own legal practice, they're just doing it, doing it, doing it.

At the same time, they want everything—freedom, respect, money. Most of all, they want to rid themselves of meddling bosses and start their own practice. That way they can be their own boss and take home all the money. These attorneys are in the throes of an entrepreneurial seizure.

Attorneys who have been praised for their finesse at litigation or their legal knowledge believe they have what it takes to run a legal practice. It's not unlike the plumber who becomes a contractor because he's a great plumber. Sure, he may be a great plumber, but it doesn't necessarily follow that he knows how to build a practice that does this work.

It's the same for an attorney. So many of them are surprised to wake up one morning and discover that they're nowhere near as equipped for owning their own practice as they thought they were.

More than any other subject, work is the cause of obsessive-compulsive behavior by attorneys.

Work. You've got to do it every single day.

Work. If you fall behind, you'll pay for it.

Work. There's either too much or not enough.

So many attorneys describe work as what they do when they're busy. Some discriminate between the work they *could* be doing as attorneys and the work they *should* be doing as attorneys.

But according to the E-Myth, they're exactly the same thing. The work you *could* do and the work you *should* do as an attorney are identical. Let me explain.

Strategic Work versus Tactical Work

Attorneys can do only two kinds of work: strategic work and tactical work.

Tactical work is easier to understand, because it's what almost every attorney does almost every minute of every hour of every day. It's called getting the job done. It's called doing business.

Tactical work includes filing, billing, answering the telephone, going to the bank, seeing clients, drafting briefs, and building a case.

The E-Myth says that tactical work is all the work attorneys find themselves doing in a legal practice to *avoid* doing the strategic work.

"I'm too busy," most attorneys will tell you.

"How come nothing goes right unless I do it myself?" they complain in frustration.

Attorneys say these things when they're up to their ears in tactical work. But most attorneys don't understand that if they had done more strategic work, they would have less tactical work to do.

Attorneys are doing strategic work when they ask the following questions:

- Why am I an attorney?
- What will my practice look like when it's done?
- What must my practice look, act, and feel like in order for it to compete successfully?
- What are the key indicators of my practice?

Please note that I said attorneys *ask* these questions when they are doing strategic work. I didn't say these are the questions they necessarily answer.

That is the fundamental difference between strategic work and tactical work. Tactical work is all about *answers:* how to do this, how to do that.

Strategic work, in contrast, is all about *questions:* What practice are we really in? Why are we in that practice? Who specifically is our practice determined to serve? When will I sell this practice? How and where will this practice be doing business when I sell it? And so forth.

Not that strategic questions don't have answers. Attorneys who commonly ask strategic questions know that once they ask such a question, they're already on their way to *envisioning* the answer. Question and answer are part of a whole. You can't find the right answer until you've asked the right question.

Tactical work is much easier, because the question is always more obvious. In fact, you don't ask the tactical question; instead, the question arises from a result you need to get or a problem you need to solve. Billing a client is tactical work. Submitting a brief or drafting a contract is tactical work. Firing an employee is tactical work. Seeing a client is tactical work.

Tactical work is the stuff you do every day in your practice. Strategic work is the stuff you plan to do to create an exceptional practice/business/enterprise.

In tactical work, the question comes from *out there* rather than *in here*. The tactical question is about something *outside* of you, whereas the strategic question is about something *inside* of you.

The tactical question is about something you *need* to do, whereas the strategic question is about something you *want* to do. Want versus need.

If tactical work consumes you:

- You are always reacting to something outside of you.
- Your practice runs you; you don't run it.
- Your employees run you; you don't run them.
- Your life runs you; you don't run your life.

You must understand that the more strategic work you do, the more intentional your decisions, your practice, and your life become. *Intention* is the byword of strategic work.

Everything on the outside begins to serve you, to serve your vision, rather than forcing you to serve it. Everything you *need* to do is congruent with what you *want* to do. It means you have a vision, an aim, a purpose, a strategy, an *envisioned* result.

Strategic work is the work you do to *design* your practice, to design your life.

Tactical work is the work you do to *implement* the design created by strategic work. Without strategic work, there is no design. Without strategic work, all that's left is keeping busy.

There's only one thing left to do. It's time to *take action*. But first, let's listen to what Robert and Sandy have to say on the subject of work.

www.michaelegerber.com/attorney

The Reason Behind the Work

Robert Armstrong
Sanford M. Fisch

Never work just for money or power.
They won't save your soul or help you sleep at night.
—Marian Wright Edelman

One of the most difficult jobs we've faced while coaching attorneys is convincing them to stop doing the work they do every day long enough to engage in work they have never done before.

This is what Michael Gerber calls "working on the business" as opposed to "in the business."

Yet, even though it might sound good in theory, getting an attorney to actually put down the depositions so we can talk about brainstorming for the future is akin to pulling teeth. It reminds us of the Civil War general in the now-famous cartoon as he oversees his troops during a heated gun battle. Standing next to those soldiers firing the old nineteenth-century rifles is a salesman pointing to the new, automatic Gatling gun. But the general can't be bothered—the caption reads, "Not now, can't you see I'm busy?!"

Like the Gatling gun, strategic work will completely change how your firm fights the battles each and every day. For example, we see attorneys who are stressed out about having no time, yet are engaged in countless everyday activities from taking routine phone calls to acting as the firm's IT guy when a computer problem arises. We see attorneys who believe they are the only one qualified to order office supplies or proof the letterhead on new stationery, and we even met one experienced lawyer who insisted that he make the coffee every morning and pick up the daily mail.

Strategic work in this area requires that you examine all the tasks in your firm and delegate everything that does not require the attorney/owner's attention to someone else in your office. The key to making this work is a delegation system that makes sure the things that need to get done are accomplished by a properly trained staff.

Taking these principles to heart, we were able to revolutionize estate planning law firms by creating and installing systems that were managed by well-trained paralegals—systems that took the burden off the attorney and redistributed the workload in a more efficient manner. Many feared that relinquishing control would diminish the client experience, yet what actually happened was that service improved and the staff was energized.

Unexamined beliefs that these jobs had to be done by attorneys have ruled our profession, until one day we asked, "Why?" There was no legal mandate. It was the tyranny of tradition. We looked at industries and professions outside of the law for inspiration. If well-trained nurses can provide quality medical care in a physician's office, why can't we do the same for lawyers? In fact, no patient thinks twice about the services a nurse provides before you get to see the doctor.

We found that it was all about creating new client expectations, one of the many benefits of strategic work. Once you really understand the nature of strategic work, it changes everything.

In the last chapter, Michael noted that while tactical work was all about answers, strategic work was all about questions.

Questions that examine the "why" behind a particular task or function rather than just the "how." Michael also noted that when attorneys ask these strategic questions, they are on their way to "envisioning" the answers and this is where we really want you to put your focus.

Stop looking at what your firm is now, and instead, see your firm as you'd like it to be. The only way to figure out what strategic questions to ask is to determine how far away your current practice is from the practice you've envisioned. When you can see the differences, you'll know the questions to ask, and what's more, you'll be able to see the answers as well.

The result is a whole host of new and exciting possibilities that allow you to actually create something bigger than the case files you're working on now.

Your view of not only your practice, but of the legal profession itself will be seen through a different lens. You are now an architect of a business that reflects your dreams, values, and purpose, perhaps for the first time in your career.

www.michaelegerber.com/attorney

On the Subject
of Taking Action

Michael E. Gerber

Everything you want is out there waiting for you to ask.
Everything you want also wants you.
But you have to take action to get it.

—Jack Canfield

I t's time to get started, time to take action. Time to stop thinking about the old practice and start thinking about the new practice. It's not a matter of coming up with better practices; it's about reinventing the practice of law.

And the attorney has to take personal responsibility for it. That means attorneys have to be interested. They cannot abdicate accountability for the practice of law, the administration of law, or the finance of law.

Although the goal is to create systems into which attorneys can plug reasonably competent people—systems that allow the practice to run without them—attorneys must take responsibility for that happening.

I can hear the chorus: "But we're attorneys. We shouldn't have to know about this. It's beneath us." And to that I say: "Of course you should!"

All too often, as we've discussed, attorneys take no responsibility for the business of law but instead delegate tasks without any understanding of what it takes to do them, without any interest in what their people are actually doing, without any sense of what it feels like to be at the front desk when a client comes in and has to wait for forty-five minutes, and without any appreciation for the entity that is creating their livelihood.

Attorneys can open the portals of change in an instant. All you have to do is say, "I don't want to do it that way anymore." Saying it will begin to set you free—even though you don't yet understand what the practice will look like after it's been reinvented.

This demands an intentional leap from the known into the unknown. It further demands that you live there—in the unknown—for a while. It means discarding the past, that is, everything you once believed to be true.

Think of it as soaring rather than plunging.

Thought Control

You should now be clear about the need to organize your thoughts first, and then your business. Because the organization of your thoughts is the foundation for the organization of your business.

If we try to organize our business without organizing our thoughts, we will fail to attack the problem.

We have seen that organization is not simply time management. Nor is it people management. Nor is it tidying up desks or alphabetizing client files. Organization is first, last, and always cleaning up the mess of our minds.

By learning how to *think* about the practice of law, by learning how to *think* about our priorities, and by learning how to *think* about our lives, we prepare ourselves to do righteous battle with the forces of failure.

Right thinking leads to right action—and now is the time to take action. Because it is only through action that we can translate thoughts into movement in the real world, and, in the process, find fulfillment.

So, first we *think* about what we want to do. Then we must *do* it. Only in this way will we be fulfilled.

How do you put the principles that we've discussed in this book to work in your legal practice? To find out, accompany me down the path once more:

1. *Create a story about your practice.* Your story should be an idealized version of your legal practice, a vision of what the preeminent attorney in your field should be and why. Your story must become the very heart of your practice. It must become the spirit that mobilizes it, as well as everyone who walks through the doors. Without this story, your practice will be reduced to plain work.

2. *Organize your practice so that it breathes life into your story.* Unless your practice can faithfully replicate your story in action, it all becomes fiction. In that case, you'd be better off not telling your story at all. And without a story, you'd be better off leaving your practice the way it is and just hoping for the best.

Here are Some Tips for Organizing Your Legal Practice:

- Identify the key functions of your practice.
- Identify the essential processes that link those functions.
- Identify the results you have determined your practice will produce.
- Clearly state in writing how each phase will work.

Take it step by step. Think of your practice as a program, a piece of software, a system. It is a collaboration, a collection of processes dynamically interacting with one another.

Of course, your practice is also people.

3. *Engage your people in the process.* Why is this third step rather than the first? Because, contrary to the advice most business experts will give you, you must never engage your people in the process until you yourself are clear about what you intend to do.

The need for consensus is a disease of today's addled mind. It's a product of our troubled and confused times. When people don't know what to believe in, they often ask others to tell them. To ask is not to lead but to follow.

The prerequisite of sound leadership is first to know where you wish to go.

And so, "What do *I* want?" becomes the first question; not, "What do *they* want?" In your own practice, the vision must first be yours. To follow another's vision is to abdicate your personal accountability, your leadership role, your true power.

In short, the role of leader cannot be delegated or shared. And without leadership, no legal practice will ever succeed.

Despite what you have been told, *Win-Win* is a secondary step, not a primary one. The opposite of *Win-Win* is not necessarily *They Lose.*

Let's say "they" can win by choosing a good horse. The best choice will not be made by consensus. "Guys, what horse do you think we should ride?" will always lead to endless and worthless discussions. By the time you're done jawing, the horse will have already left the post.

Before you talk to your people about what you intend to do in your practice and why you intend to do it, you need to reach agreement with yourself.

It's important to know (1) *exactly* what you want, (2) how you intend to proceed, (3) what's important to you and what isn't, and (4) what you want the practice to be and how you want it to get there.

Once you have that agreement, it's critical that you engage your people in a discussion about what you intend to do and why. Be clear, both with yourself and with them.

The Story

The story is paramount because it is your vision. Tell it with passion and conviction. Tell it with precision. Never hurry a great story. Unveil it slowly. Don't mumble or show embarrassment. Never apologize or display false modesty. Look your audience in the eyes and tell your story as though it is the most important one they'll ever hear about business. Your business. The business into which you intend to pour your heart, your soul, your intelligence, your imagination, your time, your money, and your sweaty persistence.

Get into the storytelling zone. Behave as though it means everything to you. Show no equivocation when telling your story.

These tips are important because you're going to tell your story over and over—to clients, to new and old employees, to attorneys, to associate lawyers, to paralegals, and to your family and friends. You're going to tell it at your church or synagogue; to your card-playing or fishing buddies; and to organizations such as Kiwanis, Rotary, YMCA, Hadassah, and Boy Scouts.

There are few moments in your life when telling a great story about a great business is inappropriate.

If it is to be persuasive, you must love your story. Do you think Walt Disney loved his Disneyland story? Or Ray Kroc his McDonald's story? What about Fred Smith at Federal Express? Or Debbie Fields at Mrs. Field's Cookies? Or Tom Watson Jr. at IBM?

Do you think these people loved their stories? Do you think others loved (and *still* love) to hear them? I dare say *all* successful entrepreneurs have loved the story of their business. Because that's what true entrepreneurs do: They tell stories that come to life in the form of their business.

Remember: A great story never fails. A great story is always a joy to hear.

In summary, you first need to clarify, both for yourself and for your people, the *story* of your practice. Then you need to detail the *process* that your practice must go through to make your story become reality.

I call this the *business development process*. Others call it re-engineering, continuous improvement, reinventing your practice, or total quality management.

Whatever you call it, you must take three distinct steps to succeed:

1. *Innovation.* Continue to find better ways of doing what you do.

2. *Quantification.* Once that is achieved, quantify the impact of these improvements on your practice.

3. *Orchestration.* Once these improvements are verified, orchestrate this better way of running your practice so that it becomes your standard, to be repeated time and again.

In this way, the system works—no matter who's using it. And you've built a practice that works consistently, predictably, systematically. A practice you can depend on to operate exactly as promised, every single time.

Your vision, your people, your process—all linked.

A superior legal practice is a creation of your imagination, a product of your mind. So fire it up and get started!

An attorney is obliged by his ethical canons to represent his clients with "warm zeal." Wouldn't it be wonderful to apply that same sense of warm zeal to your own life?

I hope you agree with me that now you can. And now, I'm sure, you will. Now let's listen to what Robert and Sandy have to say about taking action.

www.michaelegerber.com/attorney

Taking Action

Robert Armstrong
Sanford M. Fisch

Trust only movement. Life happens at the level of events, not of words.
Trust movement.

—Alfred Adler

R ecently there has been a lot of new age talk about obtaining success through the law of attraction. This law says that you attract that which dominates your thoughts. In other words, whatever holds your attention the most is what will manifest in your life.

While the power of a focused mind can't be ignored, it's the second part of this philosophy that we want to highlight, and that part is action. For anything to happen, there must be movement in the direction of your dreams. In fact, not only do we believe in action, but we encourage *massive action*.

Now to be clear, the action can't be random or haphazard. Remember, it's not just that you need to climb a wall—you need to climb the right wall. We believe that the first step is to immediately set aside some time away from the distractions of the office and home life, and seriously examine what it is you want, not only for your business, but also how your business is going to serve your life.

Now I know that you've probably heard this sage advice before, but we're betting you haven't taken it to heart because here you are, still working for the business instead of the business working for you.

And we all know how that strategy turns out.

So this is going to be your first step in a new direction—your direction to be exact. To know how to get to where you want to be, you need to know where you want to go.

Once you've established what your "big picture" will be, the next issue you'll need to tackle is to develop a game plan for getting there. Fortunately, Michael Gerber provided you a perfect blueprint for this project: It's your primary aim, strategic objective and organizational strategy paradigm that he outlined in the E-Myth book.

The primary aim will guide you in setting goals and priorities for your life. The strategic objective will detail every aspect of how your practice will support those goals and priorities, giving you the life you want. It is the vivid description of every part of your firm as it will look when it's completed: What does the office look like? How many employees? What markets do you serve? What niches in those markets are you going to pursue? What is your annual revenue? What is your owner's compensation? How many days a week will you work? What is the position of your firm in the eyes of the community?

You get the idea. You need to develop a detailed picture of your future practice to which you can aspire.

The final part of this exercise is the organizational strategy and this answers the practical questions of what needs to get done and who is going to do it. If you're like most of the attorneys we've coached over the years, your organizational chart will have your name in multiple places.

But that little habit is going to change now, isn't it? You're going to start matching personalities and talents to functions within your firm so that every position in your practice is filled by a person who is perfectly suited for the job. This is your chance to wipe the slate clean and start building your firm based on your very own strategic vision.

Now you're doing real entrepreneurial work. There isn't a tactic in sight at this point.

But beware! This is not a trivial project and it isn't one of those "when I get around to it" kind of jobs. It requires a clear decision and solid intention to build the practice of your dreams, so don't be surprised if it takes several large blocks of your time spread out over several weeks.

In fact, take as long as you need to get it right. Just get started now.

And while it would seem that an office brainstorming session would be an appropriate event in this exercise, don't do it—at least, not yet.

While you're crafting your primary aim, you want it to be "all you"—this is after all, your vision of your firm. As you move to the strategic objective and organizational strategy, you can bring in the other owners or partners of the firm if you have them. But remember, all of this strategic planning should be done in a spirit of adventure and creativity, one that addresses the big picture as a whole rather than a checklist for micromanaging every little task in your office.

In fact, the word "strategic" comes from the Greek word "strategos," which means general. And if you consider the job of the military general, you know that he is responsible for organizing the troops and creating a battle plan—not planning the specific tasks of each soldier.

And we've been where you are now. We remember the day, more than twenty years ago, when we started this same process and decided to take those massive actions that we're asking you to take now. These actions that changed our lives and our fortunes.

It was the day that each of us finished reading the original E-Myth book by Michael Gerber, and realized that although we had experienced growth and success, we were operating in chaos and needed to make fundamental changes.

And this is how we did it: First, we separated and worked individually on our primary aims. What did we really want for our lives? Then we came together and worked out our strategic objective, our vision of our firm in as much detail as possible, and finally created our master organizational strategy, complete with a chart with all the essential positions.

In anticipation of all of us coming together as a firm, we provided a copy of the E-Myth book to all members of our staff and asked them to read it carefully in preparation for a firm retreat.

Following a successful offsite retreat in which everyone fully participated, we finalized our blueprint. We were now all looking at the practice with new eyes. This allowed us to refine, and in some cases to create from scratch, systems for every task in the law firm.

Over the years, this basic powerful formula has played itself out in firms across the country. In every case it has accelerated the transformation of the individual practice into a business that served the priorities of the owner attorneys.

This is a necessary part of your journey—don't skip over it.

You may find that you are a little hesitant to instigate big changes in your practice. We know. . . . We've been there.

In fact, one of the biggest hurdles that we've seen as attorneys embark on this process is the paralysis that comes from the fear of making the wrong choice or taking the wrong path.

This fear usually stems from prior business decisions gone bad, and goodness knows, we don't want to walk down that road again. But we also know from both our own personal experience as well as that of countless others embarking on this journey, that the decision to undertake this project turned out to be the most important business decision of their lives.

It's been said that all of your problems in life can be attributed to filing mistakes. If you can represent the past, present, and future as giant filing cabinets, then you can see how our lives are adversely affected when the wrong "file" ends up in the wrong cabinet.

And that's often what we tend to do with our life experiences. Instead of placing them in the "past" filing cabinet, we tuck them away in the cabinet marked "future," where they continue to influence our every move.

Instead of looking forward to the array of possibilities that await us, we see our failures and rejections of the past staring us down, daring us to move. But move you must.

The very foundation of the American legal system is changing before our eyes. No longer can we safely rely on the traditional practice models of the past. The legal industry is changing with, or without you.

The expectations of clients in the delivery of legal services is also under attack. Face-to-face meetings are being replaced by emails and phone calls, and as our access to digital tools continues to grow, these issues will occur far more often. The power of the Internet, along with the digital revolution, is being felt in every specialty, in every practice, in every area of the country.

The reaction to all this change will frighten some and motivate others. We prefer to be one of the latter. We see these developments as the opportunities of a lifetime for law firms that are prepared.

What is clear is that you are now standing on uncertain ground. The future is not written in stone and you have the option of painting it the way you see fit.

But before you can have a business that serves your needs, the work you do in your firm must leave you feeling fulfilled and energized rather than exhausted and overworked. Managing a practice by gritting your teeth and toughing it out will never give you a career that lights you up, regardless of how much money is dumped in your lap. We've found that taking the time to discover your natural strengths and talents and then delegating everything else is a recipe for a prosperous firm.

Interestingly, most attorneys we've met give us a blank look when we ask what it is they really like to do, because no one ever asked that question before. They just assumed that you throw yourself at every challenge in the firm and recognize that you have to take the bad with the good.

We're here to tell you that not only can you avoid the things you hate, but that by doing them, you're actually slowing your own progress. The sad truth is that all of us in this culture have been taught to lightly acknowledge our strengths but to really "work" on our weaknesses. Don't believe it? The next time your child comes home from school waving a report card, consider which grades you comment on first. Do you simply focus on the A's and B's, or are you more concerned with the C's, D's, and F's?

It happens all the time, no matter what age you are or how much money you might make. We honestly believe that our efforts should be devoted to those areas where we perform poorly. After all, that's what "self-improvement" is all about, right?

But research shows that it's actually far more effective and productive to work on your strengths, those innate talents that are part of our natural wiring and represent the areas in which we excel.

And when we spend our time doing these tasks, we feel energized, not drained. We look forward to getting started, and we're never watching the clock to see when we can stop.

Fortunately, identifying your talents isn't as difficult as you might think. There are two wonderful, easily accessible and reasonably priced tests you can take that will quickly show you the powerful undistinguished talents that have been shaping your life since childhood.

The first is the Kolbe A™ Index, a test you can take online for about $50. According to the company's web site, "IQ tests tell you what you can do. Personality tests tell you what you want to do. . . . The Kolbe A™ Index measures what you WILL or WON'T do. This quick and easy 36-question instrument gives you greater understanding of your own natural instincts and allows you to begin the process of maximizing your potential."

The second test is found in a $20 book called *StrengthsFinder 2.0*, by Tom Rath. It contains the collected wisdom of thousands of interviews done by the prestigious Gallup Group. The test provides five top themes that identify your natural strengths.

According to the Gallup Group, "[O]ur studies indicate that people who *do* have the opportunity to focus on their strengths every day are *six times as likely to be engaged in their jobs and more than three times as likely to report having an excellent quality of life in general.*"

What we're asking you to do is figure out what it is that you "want" to do and start delegating the items that don't fit with your natural talents. "Refile" those misplaced folders in your life and create a vision of possibility in your firm. Forget about the limitations of the past—instead, use your present to create a future that truly represents what you want—not just from a business perspective but from your life as well.

So now you've heard our story. We hope that reading this book becomes your defining moment and is the bridge you need to take you from where you are now to where you want to be—to where you deserve to be.

Now is the perfect time to create your story, tell it to others and most importantly, live it day to day.

We are confident that if you follow these principles you will get there. Of course, we are here to help. Contact us for more information and resources at www.michaelegerber.com/attorney.

And one last thing, we hope that someday you'll give this book to another attorney and write, "Read, re-read, it changed my life . . . enjoy."

www.michaelegerber.com/attorney

AFTERWORD

eaders finding themselves at the end of a book often wonder
what to do next. If this book has moved you as we intended it
to—that is, if you now have a clearer understanding of
what's missing in your legal practice and why it is so important to
grow beyond your present state, if you are moved to the point where
you simply can't continue "doing it, doing it, doing it, busy, busy,
busy" any longer, without a higher purpose, a larger aim, a more
significant reason for being an attorney, a more productive way of
living your professional life—then here is what I recommend:

- First, come visit us at www.michaelegerber.com/attorney.

- Second, take advantage of the several options that we—Sandy,
  Robert, and I—have made available to you there. Join a tele-
  conference with us. Come to a Dreaming Room. Request more
  information about our many exciting programs through which
  you can do exactly what Robert and Sandy have done on behalf
  of hundreds of attorneys, and what I have done through the
  E-Myth Mastery Program, the Dreaming Room, Awakening the
  Entrepreneur Within coaching, and many others too numerous
  to list here. You'll find them all at www.michaelegerber.com/
  attorney. Go there now while the mood moves you.

- Third, to immediately discover a deeper sense of purpose, a
  clearer connection with all of the points we've made in this

book, call us at 760-752-7912, and ask for a meeting with Robert and Sandy, or me. We're on a mission to transform the world, along with all our other Michael E. Gerber Partners, each of whom has become an E-Myth leader in his or her industry. Hundreds more are joining us in this mission, as E-Myth books are being planned for many vertical markets throughout the world—financial advisors, accountants, chiropractors, physicians, dentists, contractors, engineers, graphic designers, sign makers, plumbers, electricians, you name it. As we move forward, more and more E-Myth experts will tell how they have transformed their business using the E-Myth point of view to guide them, and, in the process transformed their lives as well.

The important message to understand is that you can do this. You can emulate these leaders. You can grow your practice without all the turmoil and guesswork that typically consumes an attorney working on his or her own, or with others, trying to figure it all out. The point is we have figured it out. And that's what this book has been telling you.

There is an easier way, a better way, a more significant way to grow a legal practice, to grow it into a thriving business, and to grow that thriving business into a profoundly important enterprise.

Let us help you, today.

To your future, and the future of law,

Our Best,

Michael E. Gerber
Robert Armstrong
Sanford M. Fisch
www.michaelegerber.com/attorney